a commentary on john • STEWART CUSTER

I0804566

the Divine SON of GOD

BOB JONES
UNIVERSITY PRESS
Greenville, South Carolina

Library of Congress Cataloging-in-Publication Data

Custer, Stewart, 1931–
The divine Son of God : a commentary on John / Stewart Custer.
p. cm.
Includes bibliographical references.
Summary: "A devotional commentary on the Gospel of John"—Provided by publisher.
ISBN 978-1-60682-186-2 (perfect bound pbk. : alk. paper)
1. Bible. N.T. John—Commentaries. I. Title.
BS2615.53C87 2011
226.5'077—dc22

2011002561

Cover Photo Credits: Craig Oesterling

The Divine Son of God: A Commentary on John

Stewart Custer, PhD

Design by Craig Oesterling
Page Layout by Michael Boone

Greenville, South Carolina 29614
Bob Jones University Press is a division of BJU Press

Printed in the United States of America

ISBN 978-1-60682-186-2

15 14 13 12 11 10 9 8 7 6 5 4 3 2 1

Dedicated to
the memory of
my dear wife,
Carol

Contents

Preface to the Reader

This commentary has been my intention ever since I finished my commentary on Matthew (2005). The Synoptic Gospels present a unified portrait of the Lord Jesus Christ. John, however, presents a striking series of remarkable insights and revelations of the power and glory of Christ, the divine Son of the living God. He deliberately omits material that the other Gospels have already revealed. He deliberately begins with the Divine Word in eternity past and contrasts the divine-human natures of Christ in chapter after chapter of his Gospel. He describes how the Lord could create matter at will (2:3–11) and could weep at the death of a friend (11:35). He describes the glorious triumphal entry (12:12–16) and the Lord's last words to the betrayer (13:27). He gives the longest description of the Upper Room Discourse (14–16) and the only description of the great High-Priestly Prayer (17). He concludes his Gospel with the admission that he has left many things unrecorded, but he adds that if someone tried to record everything the Lord did, "even the world itself could not contain the books that should be written" (21:25*b*).

Abbreviations

EDBT—*Evangelical Dictionary of Biblical Theology*. W. A. Elwell, ed. Grand Rapids: Baker Books, 1996.

ISBE—*The International Standard Bible Encyclopedia*. 4 vols. Grand Rapids: Eerdmans, 1979–88.

NDBT—*New Dictionary of Biblical Theology*. Alexander, Rosner, Carson, Goldsworthy, eds. Downers Grove, IL: InterVarsity Press, 2000.

NT—The New Testament.

OT—The Old Testament.

p., pp.—Page, pages.

v., vv.—Verse, verses.

ZPEB—*Zondervan Pictorial Encyclopedia of the Bible*. 5 vols. Grand Rapids: Zondervan, 1975.

Introduction to John

The author. John the Apostle. Conservative authors uniformly defend the authorship of John the Apostle; liberal authors deny it, just as they deny the deity of Jesus Christ. However, some liberals will now make admissions such as "the traditions underlying John's Gospel may be historically more reliable than previously acknowledged" (*Oxford Companion to the Bible*, p. 374). Place names such as Bethesda (5:2) and Gabbatha (19:13) are now sites that have been identified. For conservative views see Westcott, B. F., *John*, pp. v–xxviii; Bruce, F. F., *The Gospel of John*, pp. 1–17; Godet, F., *Commentary on the Gospel of St. John*, I, pp. 29–53.

The purpose. John declares his purpose at the end of his Gospel: "But these things have been written in order that you may believe that Jesus is the Christ, the Son of God, and that believing you might have life in his name" (20:31). John plainly desires the reader to have the same fervent faith in the Lord Jesus Christ that he himself has.

The date. Godet argues for between AD 80 and 90 (*John*, I, p. 167). Westcott argues for the last ten years of the first century (*John*, p. xl). Borchert argues for a date before the second century (*John*, vol. I, pp. 91–92).

Main theme. Jesus Christ is the divine Word (1:1), the divine Son of God (3:16). The seven "I am" statements of the Lord are crucial to the understanding of His Person and work. The Lord Jesus claimed, "I am the Bread of life" (6:48); "the Light of the world" (8:12); "the Door of the sheep" (10:7); "the Good Shepherd" (10:11); "the Resurrection and the Life" (11:25); "the Way, the Truth, and the Life" (14:6); "the true Vine" (15:1). He is the only human being Who has ever had the divine right to command, "Follow me" (21:19*b*).

Other themes.

The verb *to believe* is mentioned 90 times in John's Gospel (1:7, 12, 50; 2:11, 22, 23; 3:12, 15, 16, 18, etc.).

The word *light* is linked to the Lord 21 times in John (1:4, 5, 7, 8 [2], 9; 3:19 [2], 20 [2], 21; 8:12 [2]; 9:5; 11:10; 12:35 [2], 36 [3], 46). See *ISBE*, "Light," III, pp. 134–36; *ZPEB*, "Light," III, pp. 932–34; *EDBT*, "Light," pp. 486–87.

The Lord brings *life* to mankind (1:4; 3:15, 16, 36; 4:14, 36; 5:24, 26, 29, 39, 40; 6:27, 33, 35, 40, 47, 48, 51, 53, 54, 63, 68; 8:12; 10:10, 28; 11:25; 12:25, 50; 14:6; 17:2, 3; 20:31). See *ISBE*, "Life," III, pp. 129–34; *ZPEB*, "Life," III, pp. 927–32; *EDBT*, "Life," pp. 484–86.

Being born [again] (1:13; 3:3, 4, 5, 6, 7, 8; 8:41; 9:2, 19, 20, 32, 34; 16:21; 18:37).

Truth occurs 25 times (1:14, 17; 3:21; 4:23, 24; 5:33; 8:32 [2], 40, 44 [2], 45, 46; 14:6, 17; 15:26; 16:7, 13; 17:17, 19; 18:37, 38.

The word *joy* occurs 8 times in John (3:29; 15:11 [2]; 16:20, 21, 22, 24; 17:13).

With all this emphasis on the Lord Jesus Christ, we must not forget that John uses the word *Father* 137 times in his Gospel, "the greatest number in any one book in the New Testament" (Morris, *New Testament Theology*, p. 248).

On the other end of the spectrum the word *world* is mentioned 67 times in John (1:9, 10, 29; 3:16, 17, 19; 4:42; 6:14, 33, 51; 7:4, 7; 8:12, 23, 26; 9:5, etc.).

For conservative comment on John, see *ZPEB*, "John, Gospel of," III, pp. 657–74; *ISBE*, "John, Gospel According to," II, pp. 1098–1107; *EDBT*, "John, Theology of," pp. 423–27; *NDBT*, "John," pp. 280–85; Morris, Leon, *The Cross in the New Testament*, "The Cross in the Gospel of St. John," pp. 144–79; *New Testament Theology*, "The Johannine Writings," pp. 223–97. For the commentary literature see the bibliography, pp. 107–128.

Unique elements in John.

The pre-existent state of Christ and His incarnation. 1:1–18.

The testimony of John the Baptist to the delegation from the Sanhedrin. 1:19–28.

The testimony of John the Baptist to Jesus as the Lamb of God and Messiah. 1:29–34.

The first public ministry of Jesus. 1:35–51.

The first miracle: water to wine. 2:1–12.

The first cleansing of the temple at the Passover. 2:13–22.

The meeting of Jesus with Nicodemus. 3:1–21.

John the Baptist's loyalty to Jesus. 3:22–36.
Jesus at Jacob's well in Samaria. 4:4–42.
The healing of the nobleman's son. 4:46–54.
The healing at the pool of Bethesda and the defense to the Jews. 5:1–47.
The sermon on the bread of life and the response. 6:22–66.
Jesus goes secretly to the Feast of Tabernacles. 7:2–53.
Jesus and the adulterous woman. 8:1–11.
Jesus, the Light of the world. 8:12–20.
Jesus' words to the Pharisees. 8:21–59.
Jesus heals and converts a man born blind. 9:1–41.
The parable of the good shepherd. 10:1–21.
At the Feast of Dedication the Jews try to stone Jesus. 10:22–40.
Jesus raises Lazarus from the dead. 11:1–54.
Jesus' words about certain Greeks who wished to see Him. 12:23–50.
Jesus washes the feet of His disciples. 13:1–20.
Jesus' farewell discourse to His disciples. 14:1–16:33.
Jesus' High-Priestly Prayer. 17:1–26.
The convincing of Thomas. 20:26–29.
The appearance to 7 disciples at the Sea of Galilee. 21:1–17.

Johannine ethics.

There are great similarities between the Gospel and epistles of John. The great Johannine words (life, light, love, and truth) can be found in both. John's ethics are generally theological. It is clear that God is light, and therefore His children will walk in the light and abhor the darkness. God is love, and therefore they will love God and His people. The verb "I love" (*agapao*) and the noun "love" (*agape*) occur more in John's Gospel than in all the Synoptic Gospels combined. John was "the disciple whom Jesus loved" (13:23; 19:26; 20:2; 21:7, 20). John learned his lesson well in the teaching and practice of the loving Savior. The Lord Jesus gives "a new commandment. . . , That ye love one another; as I have loved you, that ye also love one another" (13:34). There is to be a special love between the believers in the future Christian church. We have experienced the love of Christ; therefore we must let His love flow through us to others. For further discussion see Maston, T. B., *Biblical Ethics*, "The Johannine Literature," pp. 211–44; *ISBE*, "Ethics," II, pp. 164–83; *ZPEB*, "Ethics," II, pp. 385–411; *EDBT*, "Ethics," pp. 213–16.

Animals mentioned in John.

Lamb. 1:29; 21:15.
Dove. 1:32; 2:14.
Sheep. 2:15; 5:2; 10:1-3, 7, 11, 12, 26, 27; 21:16.
Oxen. 2:15.
The serpent. 3:14.
Cattle. 4:12.
Wolf. 10:12.
A young ass. 12:14, 15.
The cock. 13:38; 18:27.
Fish. 6:9, 11; 21:6, 8, 9, 10, 11, 13.

Outline of John

John testifies to the divine nature of the Lord Jesus Christ.

I. The witness to the Word of God. John 1:1–14.
II. The witness of John the Baptist. John 1:15–51.
III. The witness of the miracles. John 2.
IV. The witness to Nicodemus. John 3.
V. The witness to the Samaritan woman. John 4.
VI. The witness at the pool of Bethesda. John 5.
VII. The witness of miracles and the Bread of life. John 6.
VIII. The witness at the Feast of Tabernacles. John 7.
IX. The witness as the Light of the world. John 8.
X. The witness to the blind man. John 9.
XI. The witness of the Good Shepherd. John 10.
XII. The witness of the raising of Lazarus. John 11.
XIII. The witness of the triumphal entry and the explanation. John 12.
XIV. The witness of the last Passover. John 13.
XV. The witness of the Upper Room Discourse. John 14–16.
XVI. The witness of the High-Priestly Prayer. John 17.
XVII. The witness in the trials. John 18.
XVIII. The witness in the death. John 19.
XIX. The witness of the Resurrection. John 20–21.

Westcott provides a broad outline (*John*, pp. xlii–xliii):

I. The prologue. John 1:1–18.
II. The self-revelation of Christ to the world. John 1:19–12:50.
III. The self-revelation of Christ to the disciples. John 13–21.

ZPEB divides the Gospel:

I. Introduction. John 1:1–51.
II. Public ministry. 2:1–12:50.
III. Private conference with disciples. 13:1–17:26.
IV. Jesus is glorified. 18:1–21:25.

The Theology of John

John begins his book in eternity past with the divine Word as part of the divine nature, and with the powers of life and creation (1:1–4). He concludes his Gospel with Jesus' command to disciples to continue following Him (21:19). In the chapters between, John portrays the Lord Jesus Christ as a mighty Savior, a loving Friend of sinners, and the Redeemer of His people. He is prepared to impart the love of God to His people (3:16). He commands His people to keep on searching the Scriptures for testimony to His divine nature (5:39). His heavenly Father sent Him into the world "that the world through him might be saved" (3:17*b*).

John writes after the Synoptic Gospels (Matthew, Mark, and Luke) and hence makes no attempt to repeat the basic information that they have recorded. He emphasizes the supernatural nature of the Lord and His infinite love for fallen man.

The Doctrine of God. The word *God* occurs 74 times in the Gospel of John. The author emphasizes the doctrine of the Trinity. In the first chapter he refers to the Word (Christ), the Father (v. 14), and the Spirit (vv. 32–33). He explains that the Word was with God, and yet was God, in the same sense as the Father is God (vv. 1–2). The Spirit descended from heaven and continued abiding upon Christ (vv. 32–34).

It is the Spirit Who gives the new birth to believers (3:5–8). God's infinite love caused Him to send His only begotten Son into the world to bring believers into salvation (3:16–17). As a divine Being, God is a Spirit, and hence those who worship Him must do so in spirit and in truth (4:24). The Lord Jesus "made himself equal with God" as the Jews perceived (5:18*b*). The loving deeds of the Son display the loving nature of the Father (5:19–20). The Lord commands all men to "keep on searching the Scriptures" (5:39*a*), for they are His revelation of salvation. The Lord declared that He always did those things that please His Father (8:29*b*). The Father knows the Son perfectly, and Jesus said, "Even so know I the Father" (10:15*a*). There is perfect unity between the Father and the Son: "I and my Father, we are one" (10:30).

The Lord would not pray to His Father to spare Him from the death on the cross (12:27). Instead, He prayed, "Father, glorify thy name" (12:28*a*). The Father answered with a divine voice from heaven. Jesus cried out, "He that believeth on me, believeth not on me, but on him that sent me" (12:44). The Lord Jesus knew perfectly that "he was come from God, and went to God" (13:3*b*). The Lord urged believers to believe in Him in the same way that they believed in God the Father: "Ye believe in God, believe also in me" (14:1*b*). The Lord said, "In my Father's house are many dwelling places: if it were not so, I would have told you. I go to prepare a place for you" (14:2). The Lord said plainly, "No man cometh unto the Father, but by me" (14:6*b*). The Lord promised, "I will pray the Father, and he shall give you another Comforter, that he may abide with you for ever; even the Spirit of truth" (14:16–17*a*). The Lord also said, "If a man love me, he will keep my words: and my Father will love him, and we will come unto him, and make our abode with him" (14:23). The Lord declared, "I am the true vine, and my Father is the husbandman" (15:1). He went on to say, "Herein is my Father glorified, that ye bear much fruit; so shall ye be my disciples" (15:8). He also warned, "He that hateth me hateth my Father also" (15:23). The Lord explained that it was profitable for Him to go away, because He would send the Comforter to believers (16:7). The Lord promised that He, the Spirit, "will guide you into all truth" (16:13*a*). The Lord assured the disciples, "I came forth from the Father, and am come into the world: again, I leave the world, and go to the Father" (16:28).

The Father, the Son, and the Holy Spirit make up the one true God as the Lord taught in the Great Commission (Matt. 28:18–20). John's Gospel provides a great expansion of this doctrine. For thorough discussion of the Trinity see Bavinck, Herman, *The Doctrine of God*, "The Holy Trinity," pp. 255–336; Augustine, *Basic Writings of St. Augustine*, 2 vols., Whitney J. Oates, ed. (New York: Random House, 1948), vol. 2, *On the Trinity*, pp. 665–898; Warfield, Benjamin Breckinridge, *Biblical and Theological Studies*, "The Biblical Doctrine of the Trinity," pp. 22–59; for a popular explanation see Kaiser, Davids, Bruce, and Brauch, *Hard Sayings of the Bible*, "One God or Three," pp. 490–92.

The Names and Titles of Christ. The names and titles manifest the different facets of His character. They manifest both the human and the divine natures of Christ.

1. Jesus (235 times in John). Twice the compound name "Jesus Christ" occurs (1:17; 17:3). "Jesus of Nazareth" occurs 4 times (1:45; 18:5, 7; 19:19). The other 229 times "Jesus" is used alone (1:29, 36, 37, 38, 42, 43, 47, 48, 50, etc.). See *ZPEB*, "Jesus Christ," III, pp. 497–583; *ISBE*, "Jesus Christ," II, pp. 1034–49; *EDBT*, "Jesus Christ," pp. 396–406; *NDBT*, "Jesus Christ," pp. 592–602.
2. Son (43 times). "Son of God" occurs 9 times (1:34, 49; 3:18; 5:25; 10:36; 11:4, 27; 19:7; 20:31). "Son of man" occurs 13 times (1:51; 3:13, 14; 5:27; 6:27, 53, 62; 8:28; 9:35; 12:23, 34 [2]; 13:31). "The Son" occurs 18 times (3:17, 35, 36 [2]; 5:19 [2], 20, 21, 22, 23 [2], 26; 6:40; 8:35, 36; 14:13; 17:1 [2]. "Son of Joseph" occurs twice (1:45; 6:42). "Only begotten" or "unique Son" occurs 3 times (*monogenes huios*, 1:14; 3:16, 18).
3. "Christ," the anointed One, the Messiah, occurs 8 times, twice with "Jesus" (see above) and alone once (1:41). "The Christ" occurs 5 times (7:26, 31, 41; 11:27; 20:31). Once Jesus claimed the title without using it (4:26). Sometimes people mention the office without meaning Jesus (10:24; 12:34).
4. Messiah (1 time, 1:41).
5. Lord (35 times). It is used 8 times as a narrative designation (4:1; 6:23; 11:2; 20:18, 20, 25; 21:7, 12). The other 27 times people either speak of Him or address Him as Lord (6:68; 9:36, 38; 11:3, 21, 27, 32, 39; 13:6, 9, 13, 14, 25, 36, 37; 14:5, 8, 22; 20:2, 13, 28; 21:7, 15, 16, 17, 20, 21). See *ISBE*, "Lord," III, pp. 157–58; *ZPEB*, "Lord (Christ)," III, pp. 959–60; *EDBT*, "Jesus Christ, Name and Titles of," *Lord*, pp. 409–10.
6. The Light (18 times). "The light" occurs 14 times (1:4, 5, 7, 8; 3:19 [2], 20 [2], 21. "The true Light" occurs once (1:9), "the Light of the world" occurs twice (8:12; 9:5); the "Light of life" occurs once (8:12). Contrast John, the lamp (5:35).
7. King (13 times). "King of Israel" twice (1:49; 12:13); "King of the Jews" (18:33, 39; 19:3, 19, 21 [2]; "King" (12:15; 18:37 [2]; 19:14, 15).
8. The Word (*Logos*, 4 times). 1:1 [3], 14. Compare John 17:17. See *ZPEB*, "Word, Word of the Lord," V, pp. 956–62; *ISBE*, "Word," IV, pp. 1101–7; *EDBT*, "Word," pp. 828–31; *NDBT*, "Word," pp. 848–53.

9. The Lamb of God (2 times). John the Baptist calls Him this (1:29, 36).
10. God (3 times). "Unique God," or "only begotten" (1:18). "My God" is Thomas's cry (20:28). The people say He made Himself God (10:33). Thomas calls Him "my God" (20:28).
11. Man (12 times). "A man" (4:29; 8:40; 9:11; 10:33; 11:50; 18:14); "this man" (9:16, 24; 11:47; 18:17, 29); "the man" (19:5).
12. Rabbi (7 times, 1:38, 49; 3:2; 4:31; 6:25; 9:2; 11:8).
13. Rabbouni (1). Mary alone calls Him "my Master" (20:16).
14. Teacher, Master (6 times, 1:38; 3:2; 11:28; 13:13, 14; 20:16).
15. Bridegroom (3 times, all in 3:29).
16. Prophet (5 times). "A prophet" (4:19, 44; 9:17); "the prophet" (6:14; 7:40).
17. The Savior of the world (1 time, 4:42).
18. The Holy One of God (1 time, 6:69).
19. I am (1 time, 8:58).
20. The Bread (7). The bread of God (6:33); the bread of life (6:35, 48); the bread which comes down from heaven (6:41, 50, 58); the living bread (6:51).
21. The door (2). "I am the door" (10:9); "I am the door of the sheep" (10:7).
22. The Good Shepherd (3 times, 10:11 [2], 14).
23. The Resurrection and the Life (1 time, 11:25).
24. The Way, the Truth, and the Life (1 time, 14:6).
25. The Vine (2). "The Vine" (15:5); "The True Vine" (15:1).

For John's theology see *ZPEB*, "Johannine Theology," III, pp. 623–36; *ISBE*, "Johannine Theology," II, pp. 1081–91; *EDBT*, "John, Theology of," pp. 423–27; *NDBT*, "John," pp. 280–85.

The Holy Spirit. John the Baptist testifies that he saw the Spirit descending from heaven like a dove and remaining upon the Lord Jesus (1:32–33). That was a sign to John that the Lord Jesus was the One Who baptized with the Spirit. The Lord Jesus taught that a man must be born of water and of the Spirit to enter into the kingdom of God (3:5). He went on to explain that the action of the Spirit is very different from physical processes (3:6–8). God the Father does not give the Spirit by measure to the Lord Jesus. The Father gives all things to the Son (3:35). Believers must worship the Father in Spirit and in truth (4:24). It is the Spirit Who makes alive (6:63). The Lord prophesied that the Spirit would flow through believers (7:38). The Lord called the Comforter the Spirit of truth (14:16–17). The Lord Jesus taught clearly that "when the Comforter is come, whom I will send unto you from the Father, even the Spirit of truth, which proceedeth from the Father, he shall testify of me" (15:26). The Lord went on to teach that "when he, the Spirit of truth, is come, he will guide you into all truth: for he shall not speak of himself; but whatsoever he shall hear, that shall he speak: and he will shew you things to come" (16:13).

The Doctrine of Sin. John the Baptist introduced the Lord Jesus to the people by declaring, "Behold the Lamb of God, which taketh away the sin of the world" (1:29*b*). The Lord Jesus warned the people, "I said therefore unto you, that ye shall die in your sins: for if ye believe not that I am, ye shall die in your sins" (8:24). If they did not believe in His divine power to forgive sin, they would die in their sins. No other person can forgive sin. The Lord went on to say, "Verily, verily, I say unto you, Whosoever keeps on committing sin is the slave of sin" (8:34). The Lord also declared that the Holy Spirit would convict the world "of sin, because they believe not on me" (16:9). Thus the ministry of the Holy Spirit is to convict men of that very sin of unbelief in the Lord Jesus (16:8–9). If men were really morally blind, they would have no sin, "but now ye say, We see; therefore your sin remaineth" (9:41*b*). There are definitely degrees of sin and punishment (19:11).

The Doctrine of Satan. Satan is that fallen angel who tempted Adam and Eve in the garden of Eden (Gen. 3:1–14) and who tempted Job to desert the Lord (Job 1:6–12). He had the temerity to tempt the Lord Jesus Christ Himself (Matt. 4:1–11). The Lord Jesus warned against his lies and deceptions (John 8:44; 13:27). Note the prophecy of Satan's final destination (Rev. 20:1–10). For further study see Chafer, L. S., *Satan*; Pentecost, D., *Your Adversary the Devil*; Elwell, *EDBT*, "Satan," pp. 714–15.

The Doctrine of Salvation. John emphasizes the doctrine of salvation. Every person needs to get right with God by faith in the Savior, Jesus Christ. He stresses that as many as receive the Lord Jesus Christ as Savior receive the authority to become sons of God: they are born of God (1:12–13). Christ is the Lamb of God Who takes away the sin of the world (1:29). A sinful man needs to be born again (3:5–7). God loved the world enough to send His dear Son to die for the sins of mankind (3:16). The Lord commanded, "Keep on searching the scriptures; for in them ye think ye have eternal life: and they are they which testify of me" (5:39). Salvation can be found only in Christ. He promised, "And this is the will of him that sent me, that every one which seeth the Son, and believeth on him, may have everlasting life: and I will raise him up at the last day" (6:40). "Verily, verily, I say unto you, He that believeth on me hath everlasting life" (6:47). "If any man thirst, let him come unto me, and drink. He that believeth on me, as the scripture hath said, out of his belly shall flow rivers of living water" (7:37*b*, 38). "I am the light of the world: he that followeth me shall not walk in darkness, but shall have the light of life" (8:12). "Verily, verily, I say unto you, I am the door of the sheep" (10:7*b*). We must remember that the shepherd put down his bedroll in the doorway of the fold; there was no other door. He himself was the door. The Lord Himself protects His people. Jesus said, "I am the resurrection, and the life: he that believeth in me, though he were dead, yet shall he live: and whosoever liveth and believeth in me shall never die" (11:25–26*a*). "I am the way, the truth, and the life: no man cometh unto the Father, but by me" (14:6*b*). The Lord also prayed in the great High-Priestly Prayer, "Neither pray I for these alone, but for them also which shall believe on me through their word" (17:20). The verb *to pray* occurs 6 times in John (4:31; 14:16; 16:26; 17:9, 15, 20), but the noun *prayer* does not occur at all. John tells us plainly what his theme is: "And many other signs truly did Jesus in the presence of his disciples, which are not written in this book: but these are written, that ye might believe that Jesus is the Christ, the Son of God; and that believing ye might have life through his name" (20:30–31). Plainly John has treasured up the teaching of the Lord Jesus Christ that He alone is the means of salvation for His people. There is none other who can save from sin.

The Ethics of Jesus. The Lord Jesus was among the disciples "as one who serves." The example of the "foot washing" is obvious (13:1–17). The Lord provided wine at the wedding in Cana of Galilee (2:3–11). Contrary to custom, He talked with the Samaritan woman to bring her to God (4:24–29). He commanded, "Keep on searching the Scriptures" (5:39*a*). He forgave the adulterous woman (8:7–11). He was devoted to always pleasing His Father (8:29). He claimed, "I am the good shepherd: the good shepherd giveth his life for the sheep" (10:11). He declared, "If any man serve me, let him keep on following me" (12:26*a*). He also said, "Ye call me Master and Lord: and ye say well; for so I am. If I then, your Lord and Master, have washed your feet; ye also ought to wash one another's feet" (13:13–14). "As the Father hath loved me, so have I loved you: continue ye in my love" (15:9). His final command to Peter is still ours: "Keep on following me" (21:19*b*). For discussion see *ISBE*, "Ethics: of Jesus; NT Ethics," II, pp. 169–83; *ZPEB*, "Ethics of Jesus," II, pp. 404–11; *EDBT*, "Ethics," pp. 213–16; *Holman Bible Dictionary*, "Ethics," pp. 441–44.

Mastering the Book of John

The believer in the Lord Jesus Christ must not be satisfied with a shallow knowledge of Scripture. We are commanded to "search the scriptures" (John 5:39*a*), meditate on them day and night (Josh. 1:8), and use them for doctrine, reproof, correction, and instruction in righteousness (II Tim. 3:16). It is a good thing for a Christian to study Scripture the way God wrote: one book at a time. It is also good to study so as to digest and absorb that content and the great biblical truths that are in it ("Thy words were found, and I did eat them," Jer. 15:16*a*). The reader should come to the Gospel of John with the determination to learn what is in it and to apply its teaching to the life that he lives. He should know the outline of John; he should have a theme to characterize each chapter; he should know each person, place, and major doctrine that is found in each chapter. He should certainly apply the teaching to his own heart relationship with his Savior. The Lord Jesus invited us, "Come unto me, all ye that labour and are heavy laden, and I will give you rest" (Matt. 11:28), but He also added, "Take my yoke upon you, and learn of me; for I am meek and lowly in heart: and ye shall find rest unto your souls" (Matt. 11:29). Let us pray the Lord that He will accomplish His purpose in our souls.

JOHN 1

The Word of God Revealed

Persons

the Word, Jesus Christ
God the Father
John the Baptist
Jews
priests and Levites
Pharisees
the Holy Spirit
Andrew
Simon Peter (Cephas)
Philip
Nathanael

Persons mentioned

believers
Moses
the Messiah
Elijah
the promised Prophet (Deut. 18:15)
Isaiah
two of John's disciples
Joseph
the angels of God
the Son of man

Places mentioned

the world
Jerusalem
the wilderness
Bethabara (Bethany)
Jordan
Galilee
Bethsaida
Nazareth
Heaven

Doctrines taught

the Trinity: the Father, the Word, and the Holy Spirit
Jesus the Word is God
creation of all things by God
the law
grace
truth
baptism
Jesus the Son of God
Jesus the true Light
The Word was made flesh
Jesus the Lamb of God
taking away the sin of the world
Jesus the Messiah
Jesus the King of Israel
witnessing for Christ
angels
Jesus the Son of man

John 1 Exposition

I. The Word Revealed. vv. 1–14.

"In the beginning was the Word, and the Word was with God, and the Word was God" (1:1). John begins his Gospel with God. God is not a monistic block. God is a Trinity of three Persons: Father, Son, and Spirit. Matthew teaches the same doctrine (Matt. 28:19), as does Paul (II Cor. 13:14). The Spirit is not a neutral Being; He is the Holy Spirit (John 1:33). Since there has always been personal, loving, fellowship between the Persons, there is a logical reason for God to love the world that He created (3:16). Love is an integral part of the nature of God. It is natural for God to reach out to help and bless His creation. In the beginning God was there. He is the origin of all that exists. The Word, Jesus Christ, was the Agent of creation. "All things were made by him" (v. 3). Christ is the Origin of all life (v. 4). God caused His light to shine forth in the universe. The stars and galaxies are His creation. His light shines in the darkness of a sin-cursed world, but the world does not see Him (v. 5).

John the Baptist came to be a witness to the Lord as the light (vv. 6–8). The Lord Jesus Christ is the true Light Who provides spiritual illumination to every person (v. 9). Although He created the world, its people do not

---

1:1. *Word* is the Greek *logos*, something thought or spoken. In this context it is used as a title of the Lord Jesus Christ. It implies the full deity of the Lord Jesus (v. 14). He is the utterance [message] of God to mankind. *Logos* must be sharply distinguished from *rema*, a grammatical word (see Custer, *A Treasury of New Testament Synonyms*, pp. 78–82). Borchert argues "that the Prologue contains some of the most tightly reasoned patterns of theological reflection in the New Testament" (*John 1–11*, p. 101). For discussion see *ZPEB*, "Logos," III, pp. 953–58; *ISBE*, "Word," IV, pp. 1101–7; *EDBT*, "Word," pp. 828–31; *NDBT*, "Word," pp. 848–53; Harrison, R. K., ed., *The New Unger's Bible Dictionary*, "Logos," p. 780.

The word *God* occurs 83 times in the Greek text of John's Gospel.

1:3. The Lord Jesus Christ was the Agent of creation. He was the One Who said, "Let there be" (Gen. 1:3, 6, 14, etc.). He is also the Agent of life for His people (1:4; 3:15; 4:14).

1:4–9. The Lord Jesus Christ is the Source of light for His people. In Christ people find the Light of truth and salvation. See *ZPEB*, "Light," III, pp. 932–34; *ISBE*, "Light," III, pp. 134–36; *EDBT*, "Light," pp. 486–87; *NDBT*, "Light," pp. 644–46; Harrison, E. F., ed., *Baker's Dictionary of Theology*, "Light," p. 324.

1:7. The purpose of John is to bring his readers to believe in the Lord Jesus Christ as the Savior of the world. Note his use of the word *believe* (98 times in the Gospel of John: see 1:7, 12, 50; 2:11, 22, 23; 3:12, 15, 16, 18, 36; 4:21, 39, 41, 42, 48, 50, 53; 5:24, 38, 44, 46, etc.). See also v. 12, "Faith."

1:9. The word *world* (*kosmos*) occurs 78 times in John (1:9, 10, 29, 3:16, etc.).

understand their need of His salvation (v. 10). He came to His own people (the Jews), but they did not receive Him as their messianic King (v. 11). But the Lord Jesus Christ has opened the door of salvation to all who will believe in Him. "As many as received him, to them he gave authority to become children [born ones] of God, the ones believing in his name" (v. 12). The person who receives the Lord Jesus Christ as his Savior from sin is "born again" with spiritual life (v. 13).

"And the Word was made flesh, and dwelt [tabernacled] among us, and we beheld his glory, glory as the only begotten of the Father, full of grace and truth" (v. 14). This is the mystery of the ages. The eternal Son of God came to earth to rescue mankind from sin by the sacrifice of Himself on the cross. John testified as an apostle to the glory that he saw in the Person of the Lord Jesus Christ.

1:11. The Lord came to the Hebrew people, but they rejected Him and crucified Him. At the second coming He will be their Deliverer, and they will receive Him (Matt. 25:31–46).

1:12. The people who believe in the Person of the Lord Jesus Christ as Savior become sons of God, members of the family of God's people. See *ZPEB*, "Faith, Faithfulness," II, pp. 479–91; *ISBE*, "Faith," II, pp. 273–75; *EDBT*, "Faith," pp. 236–39; *NDBT*, "Faith, Faithfulness," pp. 487–93.

The word *authority* occurs 8 times in John (1:12; 5:27; 10:18 [2]; 17:2; 19:10 [2], 11). See *ZPEB*, "Authority," I, pp. 420–21; *ISBE*, "Authority," I, pp. 364–71; *EDBT*, "Authority," pp. 45–46; Warfield, B. B. *The Inspiration and Authority of the Bible*, 442 pp.

1:13. The "new birth," or regeneration, is the heart of salvation for the believer in Christ. He promised eternal life to those who believe in Him (10:25–28). This new life includes cleansing from sin and restoration to the favor of God. See *ISBE*, "Regeneration," IV, pp. 67–71; *ZPEB*, "Regeneration," V, pp. 52–57; *EDBT*, "New Birth," pp. 558–59; *NDBT*, "Regeneration," pp. 720–23; Harrison, E. F., ed., *Baker's Dictionary of Theology*, "Regeneration," pp. 440–41.

1:14. "And the Word was made flesh." Here is the mystery of the Incarnation. Why would the Lord of all assume the form of a humble man? The Lord Jesus did not save mankind while He remained in the courts of heaven; He came down to the "nasty now and now" to rescue and redeem mankind as His cherished bride. For discussion see *ZPEB*, "Incarnation," III, pp. 267–74; *ISBE*, "Person of Christ," III, pp. 781–801; Harrison, R. K., ed., *The New Unger's Bible Dictionary*, "Incarnation," pp. 613–15.

1:14, 18; 3:16, 18; I John 4:9; Heb. 11:17.

The word *only begotten* occurs 4 times in John (1:14, 18; 3:16, 18). The *only begotten* (*monogenes*) is one of the very important titles of the Son of God. He is the *unique* Son of His heavenly Father. For discussion see *ZPEB*, "Only Begotten," IV, pp. 538–39; *ISBE*, "Only Begotten," III, p. 606; *EDBT*, "Jesus Christ, Name and Titles of," p. 410.

For God as the heavenly Father see *ZPEB*, "Fatherhood of God," II, pp. 505–6; *ISBE*, "God the Father," II, pp. 509–15; *EDBT*, "God," pp. 288–95; *NDBT*, "God," pp. 511–21; Bavinck,

II. The Witness of John the Baptist. vv. 15–34.

All the Gospels agree that the testimony of John the Baptist was important for the identification of the Lord Jesus Christ as the messianic King (Matt. 3:1–12; Mark 1:3–8; Luke 3:2–17; John 1:19–34). The verb used here is a historical present: "John bears witness of him," meaning that John's testimony bears witness to Christ as long as the Gospels are read. The Lord Jesus paid high tribute to John as a prophet (Luke 7:28). John would claim to be only "the voice of one crying in the wilderness, Make straight the way of the Lord" (John 1:23). The statement "No man has seen God at any time" means that the Old Testament descriptions of prophets seeing the Lord were experiences carefully veiled to protect the vision of the prophet. No one in this life has seen God in all His supernatural splendor (v. 18). John flatly denied being the Messiah or Elijah (vv. 20–21). When the Pharisees asked John why he was baptizing, he told them that he was preparing for the Messiah (vv. 26–27). When John saw the Lord coming to him, he declared, "Behold the Lamb of God, which takes away the sin of the world"

Herman, *The Doctrine of God*, "The Holy Trinity," pp. 255–334; Berkhof, L., *Systematic Theology*, "The Holy Trinity," pp. 82–99; Morey, Robert, *The Trinity*, 587 pp.

1:14, 16, 17. The word *grace* occurs three times in this context only in John's Gospel. It is one of the major doctrines in Paul (Rom. 1:5, 7, etc.). See *ISBE*, "Grace," II, pp. 547–52; *ZPEB*, "Grace," II, pp. 799–804; *EDBT*, "Grace," pp. 312–16; *NDBT*, "Grace," pp. 524–27.

The word *truth* occurs 25 times in John's Gospel (1:14, 17; 3:21; 4:23, 24; 5:33; 8:32; etc.).

1:15. For John the Baptist see *ZPEB*, "John the Baptist," III, pp. 641–47; *ISBE*, "John the Baptist," II, pp. 1108–11; Edersheim, Alfred, *The Life and Times of Jesus the Messiah*, I, pp. 255–84.

1:17. The name *Christ*, "anointed one," occurs 19 times in John's Gospel (1:17, 20, 25, 41; 3:28; 4:25, 29; 7:26, 27, 31, 41 [2], 42; 9:22; 10:24; 11:27; 12:34; 17:3; 20:31).

1:19. Jerusalem was the capital city of the land. It already had a long history of rule and influence in the area. See *ZPEB*, "Jerusalem," III, pp. 459–95; *ISBE*, "Jerusalem," II, pp. 998–1032; *EDBT*, "Jerusalem," pp. 392–96; *NDBT*, "Jerusalem," pp. 589–92; Thubron, Colin, *Jerusalem*, 200 pp.; Gafni, Shlomo S., *The Glory of Jerusalem*, 128 pp.; Mazar, Benjamin, *The Mountain of the Lord*, 303 pp.; McRay, John, *Archaeology and the New Testament*, "Herodian Jerusalem," pp. 91–127. For color photographs see Custer, *Stones of Witness*, "Within Jerusalem's Walls," pp. 114ff.

1:21. Why do they ask, "Art thou Elijah?" God had promised to send Elijah before the day of the Lord (Mal. 4:5). See *ZPEB*, "Elijah," II, pp. 284–87; *ISBE*, "Elijah," II, pp. 64–68.

1:24. For the Pharisees see *ZPEB*, "Pharisees," IV, pp. 745–52; *ISBE*, "Pharisees," III, pp. 822–29; *EDBT*, "Pharisees," pp. 607–9. They are named 19 times in John. See John 3:1; 4:1; 7:32, 45, 47, 48; etc.

1:28. Bethabara probably refers to the town of Bethany. See Westcott, *John*, p. 19, note.

(v. 29). The Lord is the fulfillment of the OT sin offering (See *ISBE*, "Sacrifices and Offerings in the OT," G. Sin Offering, IV, pp. 268f.; see also "Sin," IV, pp. 518–25). John testified, "I saw the Spirit descending from heaven like a dove, and it was remaining upon him" (v. 32). The Holy Spirit was remaining upon the Lord during the whole public ministry. John's testimony was, "I saw, and bare record that this is the Son of God" (v. 34).

III. The Work of the Lamb Begins. vv. 35–51.

The next day John the Baptist saw Jesus walking by and announced, "Behold the Lamb of God!" (v. 36). As a result, two of John's disciples followed the Lord Jesus (v. 37). John was prepared to give up all his disciples if they would follow the Lord. The Lord Jesus asked the two, "What are you seeking?" (v. 38). They address the Lord as *Rabbi*, "my master," and ask where He dwells. The Lord invited them to come and see. They did

---

1:29. What is the meaning of "the lamb of God"? The OT sacrificial lambs were types of Christ as the Lamb of God (Exod. 29:38–41). The death of Christ is the fulfillment of all the OT teaching about the need for a blood sacrifice to atone for sin. See *ZPEB*, "Lamb, Lamb of God," III, pp. 859–60; *ISBE*, "Lamb," III, pp. 61–62; *EDBT*, "Lamb, Lamb of God," pp. 460–61; *NDBT*, "Lamb," pp. 620–22.

1:32. *The Spirit* refers to the Holy Spirit. God is a Trinity: Father, Son, and Holy Spirit. See also Matt. 28:19–20; II Cor. 13:14. See also *ISBE*, "Trinity," IV, pp. 914–21; *ZPEB*, "Trinity," V, pp. 822–24; *EDBT*, "God," pp. 288–95; *NDBT*, "God," pp. 511–21; Berkhof, L., *Systematic Theology*, "The Holy Trinity," pp. 82–99; Kaiser, Davids, Bruce, and Brauch, *Hard Sayings of the Bible*, "One God or Three?" pp. 490–92. The Spirit is mentioned 17 times in John (1:32, 33 [2]; 3:5, 6, 8, 34; 4:24; 6:63; 7:39 [2]; 11:33; 14:17, 26; 15:26; 16:13; 20:22).

1:32. Why the likeness of a dove? The dove is a very gentle bird and settles on a perch with dignity.

1:33. The word *holy* occurs 5 times in John (1:33; 7:39; 14:26; 17:11; 20:22).

1:34. The title "Son of God" is applied to the Lord Jesus ten times in John (1:34, 49; 3:18; 5:25; 9:35; 10:36; 11:4, 27; 19:7; 20:31). See *ISBE*, "Son of God," IV, pp. 571–74; *ZPEB*, "Son of God," V, pp. 480–85; *EDBT*, "Jesus Christ, Name and Titles of," p. 411; *NDBT*, "Jesus Christ," pp. 592–602; Harrison, R. K., ed., *The New Unger's Bible Dictionary*, "Sonship of Christ," pp. 1211–12.

1:38. *Rabbi* was an honorific title meaning "my master." The Jews were very proud to be called by such a title. Edersheim mentions a young rabbi who knew the whole Torah and wondered when he could study Greek wisdom. His uncle reminded him of Josh. 1:8 "Thou shalt meditate therein day and night." "Consider which is the hour that is neither of the day nor of the night, and in it thou mayest study Grecian wisdom." (*Sketches of Jewish Social Life*, p. 126). For discussion see *ISBE*, "Rabbi," IV, p. 30; *ZPEB*, "Rabbi," V, p. 16; Harrison, R. K., ed., *The New Unger's Bible Dictionary*, "Rabbi," pp. 1058–59.

come and stay with Him that day. One of the two was Andrew, and he went and found his brother, Simon Peter, and told him, "We have found the Messiah" (v. 41). Andrew brought Peter to Jesus, and the Lord gave the name Cephas (Rock, Stone) to Peter (v. 42). The Lord Jesus found Philip and commanded him, "Continue following me" (v. 43). Philip in turn brings Nathanael to the Lord (vv. 45–47). Nathanael came with some doubts about the Lord, but the Lord called him an Israelite indeed. When Nathanael asked how the Lord knew him, the Lord responded, "Before that Philip called thee, when thou wast under the fig tree, I saw thee" (v. 48). When Nathanael heard that, he exclaimed, "Rabbi, thou art the Son of God; thou art the King of Israel" (v. 49). Plainly, he had been praying for the Messiah, and the Lord Jesus had heard his prayer. The Lord goes on to assure him that he would see much more in the future—"the angels of God ascending and descending upon the Son of Man" (v. 51). Westcott comments, "The divine messengers are already on the earth though we see them not; and they first bear the prayer to God before they bring down the answer from Him" (*John*, p. 28). Nathanael was going to be an observer of

---

1:40. For Andrew see *ZPEB*, "Andrew," I, pp. 156–58; *ISBE*, "Andrew," I, pp. 122–23; for Simon Peter see *ZPEB*, "Peter, Simon," IV, pp. 733–39; *ISBE*, "Peter," III, pp. 802–7; for his theology see *EDBT*, "Peter, First, Theology of," pp. 604–6.

1:41. The word *Messiah* occurs twice in John (1:41; 4:25), but the name *Christ*, "Anointed One," refers to the same office. For *Messiah* see *ZPEB*, "Messiah," IV, pp. 198–207; *ISBE*, "Messiah," III, pp. 330–38; *EDBT*, "Messiah," pp. 523–25; *NDBT*, "Jesus Christ," pp. 592–602.

1:43. For Philip see *ZPEB*, "Philip," #3, IV, p. 758; *ISBE*, "Philip the Apostle," III, p. 833.

1:45. Why did Philip call Jesus the "son of Joseph"? He was the adoptive son of Joseph and had worked in the carpenter shop for years. Nathanael had to come and meet the Lord for himself to find out how much more the Lord was. See the *Apologetics Study Bible* for more (p. 1573). For Nathanael see *ISBE*, "Nathanael," III, pp. 491–92; *ZPEB*, "Nathanael," IV, pp. 374–75.

1:45–46. Nazareth was a small commercial town with no religious history behind it. John McRay notes "Nazareth's comparative unimportance" implied by Nathaniel's remark (*Archaeology and the New Testament*, p. 157). See *ZPEB*, "Nazareth," IV, pp. 388–90; *ISBE*, "Nazareth," III, pp. 500–501; for color photographs of Nazareth see Custer, *Stones of Witness*, pp. 66–68.

1:49. The word *king* occurs 16 times in John's Gospel. The OT calls Jehovah God the King (Pss. 10:16; 20:9; 24:8; 29:10; 44:4; 47:2; 84:3). The NT calls Jesus Christ the King (Matt. 2:2; 21:5; 25:34; 27:37; John 1:49; 6:15; 12:13, 15; 18:33, 37, 39; 19:3, 12, 14, 15, 19, 21).

1:51. This is the only reference to angels in the Gospel of John. See *ZPEB*, "Angel," I, pp. 160–66; *ISBE*, "Angel," I, pp. 124–27; *EDBT*, "Angel," pp. 21–23; *NDBT*, "Spiritual Powers," pp. 796–802.

the supernatural ministry of the Lord Jesus for the next three and a half years.

Practical Applications from John 1

1. God is not a silent, "block" being; He is a Trinity, constantly communing between the Persons (1:1). Thus God desires to hear from us. When did you last pray? "Watch ye therefore, and pray always" (Luke 21:36*a*).
2. God is not to be feared (with terror), for He is the Source of light and life for men (1:4). He is to be feared with reverence. See also I Cor. 2:11–12.
3. The darkness of sin makes it difficult for mankind to "see" the Light of God (1:5).
4. True servants of God are those who are "sent" with a ministry for God (1:6).
5. Note the importance of a witness for Christ (1:7; Acts 4:33; 5:32).
6. True spiritual light comes only from Jesus Christ (1:8–9). Believers must be "children of light" (Eph. 5:8).
7. The most important Person to live on earth, the Lord Jesus, was largely ignored by the world (1:10). Worldly fame is a poor goal for any believer. "One thing have I desired of the Lord, that will I seek after; that I may dwell in the house of the Lord all the days of my life, to behold the beauty of the Lord" (Ps. 27:4*a*).
8. "The Word was made flesh, and dwelt among us . . . full of grace and truth" (1:14). How wonderful that He did not come as a warrior to crush His foes, but as a Savior to redeem a fallen, sinful people.

1:51. The title "Son of man" is one of the titles that the Lord chose to refer to Himself. See also John 3:13, 14; 5:27; 6:27, 53, 62; 8:28; 12:23, 34; 13:31. See *ISBE*, "Son of Man," IV, pp. 574–81; *ZPEB*, "Son of Man, the," V, pp. 485–86; *EDBT*, "Jesus Christ, Name and Titles of," "Son of Man," pp. 411–12.

Note the seven titles applied to the Lord Jesus in this chapter: the Word (v. 1), the true Light (v. 9), the Lamb of God (v. 29), the Son of God (v. 34), the Messiah, the Christ (v. 41), the King of Israel (v. 49), the Son of man (v. 51).

9. No man could bear the sight of the full majesty of God; Jesus Christ has revealed Him to mankind (v. 18).
10. John the Baptist never tried to make himself more than a servant of Christ (vv. 20–33).
11. John's testimony was that he was not worthy to unloose the Lord's sandal thong (1:27). That was the task of the lowliest slave in the household. How many times do believers think that some Christian work is "beneath them"?
12. John's bold testimony is no more popular today than it was in the first century (1:34).
13. How merciful is the great image of the Lamb of God (1:36). Believers really deserve the image of the Lion of the tribe of Judah for a ruler. But He is gracious.
14. How gracious that believers are known as "followers of the Lord" (1:37, 40). We should be known as slaves or soldiers. See *ISBE*, "Follow," II, pp. 326–27.
15. Andrew was quick to bring his own brother, Peter, to the Lord (vv. 40–42).
16. We should note the reality of biblical prophecy, and its power in bringing souls to the Savior (1:45–49).
17. The Lord was listening to Nathaniel's prayers (1:48ff.). We may be sure that He is listening to ours as well. (Or is He listening to our silence?)

Prayer

Dear Lord, open our eyes that we may see the true Light, and open our ears that we may hear the Word of salvation. Grant that we too may behold the Lamb of God Who takes away the sin of the world. Hear us for Jesus' sake. Amen.

JOHN 2

The Marriage at Cana

Persons

- Jesus
- mother of Jesus
- His disciples
- the servants
- the Jews
- the ruler of the feast
- the bridegroom
- His brethren
- those who sold oxen and sheep
- those who sold doves
- money changers

Places mentioned

- Cana of Galilee
- Capernaum
- Jerusalem
- the temple

Doctrines taught

- the sanctity of marriage
- the miraculous power of the Lord Jesus
- the Lord's anger against greed and avarice
- the resurrection of Christ
- the Scripture as an article of faith
- the omniscience of Jesus
- faith in Jesus

John 2 Exposition

I. The Wedding at Cana. vv. 1–11.

"And the third day there was a marriage in Cana of Galilee; and the mother of Jesus was there: and both Jesus was called, and his disciples, to the marriage" (2:1–2). The Lord Jesus did not lead a monastic life. He was there at a wedding to celebrate the occasion with the happy couple. It is not said that the mother of Jesus was invited. She was there as a friend and neighbor, helping them prepare for the occasion. She knew that the poor wine they had was quickly consumed and there was no way that they could buy any more. She said to Jesus, "They have no wine." The Lord responded rather sternly, "Woman, what have I to do with thee? mine hour is not yet come" (v. 4). He had come into the world to sacrifice Himself, not to celebrate. But Mary knew her Son very well and said to those who served, "Whatsoever he saith unto you, do it" (v. 5). She was supremely confident that He would do something to help. There were six stone waterpots standing at the door. The water in them had been used in cleaning the home in preparation for the wedding celebration. The Lord commanded those who served to fill the waterpots with water. That meant going to the well with pitchers and bringing back enough water to fill the pots. When the pots were filled, the Lord commanded them to draw out the water and bear it to the ruler of the feast. The ruler was the master of ceremonies and supervised all the feast. He had tasted the poor wine at the beginning and was astonished at the flavor of this wine. He protested that they should have brought this wine at the beginning. Those who served knew what Jesus

---

2:1. Cana was a small town, called Cana of Galilee, because there was another town named Cana as well. See *ZPEB*, "Cana of Galilee," I, p. 700; *ISBE*, "Cana," I, pp. 584–85. For archaeological background see McRay, John, *Archaeology and the New Testament*, pp. 173–75.

2:1. For *wedding* see *ZPEB*, "Marriage," IV, pp. 92–102; *ISBE*, "Marriage," III, pp. 261–66; *EDBT*, "Marriage," pp. 510–13.

2:3. Wine was a common table beverage in the ancient world, especially on festive occasions. *ISBE*, "Wine," IV, pp. 1068–72; *ZPEB*, "Wine and Strong Drink," V, pp. 935–38.

2:6. A *firkin* was about 10 gallons. See *ZPEB*, V, "Weights and Measures," Metretes, p. 918; *ISBE*, IV, "Weights and Measures," p. 1055.

2:11. Literally, "This beginning of *signs*." See also John 2:18, 23; 3:2; 4:48, 54; 6:2, 14, 26, 30; 7:31; 9:16; 10:41; 11:47; 12:18, 37; 20:30. See *ZPEB*, "Sign," V, pp. 429–31; *ISBE*, "Sign," IV, pp. 505–8; *EDBT*, "Miracle," pp. 531–34.

had done, and His disciples believed on Him (v. 11). This miracle manifested His glory, and His disciples still believe in His marvelous grace and kindness.

II. The Whip in the Temple. vv. 12–17.

"And the Jews' Passover was at hand, and Jesus went up to Jerusalem" (2:13). There He found in the temple area those that sold oxen and sheep and doves, as well as the money changers. The people could not bring their own animals to offer because inspectors would find some wart or imperfection on the animals and disqualify them for offerings. They had animals standing by that were already purified. The money changers were there because the people could not offer Roman or Greek coins (2:14). They had to offer Jewish coinage, and the money changers always got their "cut." The Lord saw the iniquitous practices and made a whip to drive the profiteers away from the temple. The temple was not there to make the crooks rich. It was there for the people to worship the heavenly Father. The disciples thought of "The zeal of thine house hath eaten me up" (2:17; Ps. 69:9).

III. The Wish for a Sign. vv. 18–25.

The Jews ask for a sign to establish the authority of Jesus (v. 18). The Lord Jesus said, "Destroy this temple, and in three days I will raise it up" (v. 19). His death and resurrection would be a staggering sign for all ages. But the people thought that He referred to the temple building. When He was risen from the dead, His disciples remembered that He had said this, and they

---

2:12. Capernaum was a city on the northwest shore of the Sea of Galilee. The Lord was there so often that it was called "his own city" (Matt. 4:13; 9:1). For photos see *ZPEB*, "Capernaum," I, pp. 746–48; *ISBE*, "Capernaum," I, pp. 609–10; Custer, *Stones of Witness*, pp. 40–43 for color photos.

2:13. The Passover was a spring festival celebrating Israel's departure from Egyptian bondage (Exod. 12:1–13). See *ZPEB*, "Passover," IV, pp. 605–11; *ISBE*, "Passover," III, pp. 675–79; *EDBT*, "Feasts and Festivals of Israel," p. 249.

2:14. For examples of ancient coinage see *ZPEB*, "Coins," I, pp. 902–11; *ISBE*, "Money," III, pp. 402–9, and color plates, pp. 396–97.

2:14–15. The people could not just bring their own animals; they had to offer ceremonially sanctified animals, of course at a high price.

2:18. What sign? The Jews were asking for a *miracle*, a *portent* to ratify His actions. But every one of the healing miracles was a sign of the Lord's divine power and authority. See *ZPEB*, "Sign," V, pp. 429–31; *ISBE*, "Sign," IV, pp. 505–8.

believed the Scripture (v. 22). It is clear that the disciples put the words of Jesus on a par with the inspired words of the Old Testament text. When He was in Jerusalem at the Passover, many people saw the miracles that He did, and believed in His name (Person). But the Lord Jesus did not commit Himself to them because He knew their hearts (vv. 24–25). They were now enthusiastic, but that could soon change.

Practical Applications from John 2

1. The marriage of a poor couple was important enough that the Lord Jesus was there. Believers need to consider how they can be an encouragement to others (Ps. 41:1). The Lord Jesus used common events, such as a wedding, to reach people for salvation (2:1).
2. It is part of the glory of the Lord to help the poor (v. 11). See Ps. 69:33.
3. Believers ought to object to religious abuses (2:14–16). God's house is not a place to make money.
4. It was only later that the disciples saw the significance of what the Lord Jesus was doing and saying (v. 17). It is a good thing for believers to meditate on the meaning of God's Word (Ps. 1:2).
5. Believers should make it a habit to remember the words of Scripture (2:22). See also Ps. 119:11.
6. The Lord Jesus knew the sinful nature of every person He dealt with, and yet He went about doing good and helping others (vv. 23–25). See Ps. 139:1–4.

Prayer

Dear Lord, prevent us from making Your house a house of merchandise. Enable us to make it a house of blessing and benefit for all who come. For Jesus' sake. Amen.

2:20. The Jews were referring to the rebuilt temple in Jerusalem. See *ZPEB*, "Temple, Jerusalem," V, pp. 622–56; *ISBE*, "Temple," IV, pp. 759–76; *EDBT*, "Temple," pp. 759–61.

2:22. The Scripture, or Scriptures, are mentioned 12 times in John (2:22; 5:39; 7:38, 42; 10:35; 13:18; 17:12; 19:24, 28, 36, 37; 20:9).

2:23. The "miracles" were literally "signs," demonstrating His divine power. See John 2:18 note.

2:25. "He was knowing," an imperfect tense, emphasizing the Lord's continual, omniscient knowing of the sinfulness of mankind. Yet He was there to help.

JOHN 3

The Testimonies of Nicodemus and John

Persons

- Nicodemus
- Jesus (the only begotten Son)
- the Father
- the Spirit

Persons mentioned

- Moses
- Jesus' disciples
- John the Baptist
- John's disciples
- the bridegroom
- the bride
- believers

Places mentioned

- Heaven
- the wilderness
- the world
- Judea
- Aenon near Salim
- the Jordan
- the earth

Doctrines taught

- miracles
- the new birth
- faith
- the kingdom of God
- the serpent in the wilderness
- the love of God
- salvation through the Son
- He that believes on the Son has everlasting life
- Men loved darkness
- doing the truth
- baptism
- He that comes from heaven is above all
- joy
- the wrath of God

John 3 Exposition

I. Nicodemus Believes. vv. 1–21.

"There was a man of the Pharisees, named Nicodemus, a ruler of the Jews" (3:1). Since he was a famous teacher himself (the premier teacher of Israel, v. 10), he came by night so that no one would see him consulting another teacher. He knew that the miracles that the Lord Jesus performed were signs from God authenticating the ministry and teaching of the Lord Jesus. He had the right opinion of the Lord Jesus, but he was not "born again." The Lord Jesus started with that very point: he needed to be "born again" (v. 3). The new birth is not merely an emotional experience; it is the transformation of character by the power of God. Unless a person is born again, he cannot enter the kingdom of God (v. 5). That which is born of the flesh is merely flesh; but that which is born of the Holy Spirit is a new spiritual being. The Lord Jesus used the wind as an illustration. People hear the sound of the wind, but they cannot see what it is doing and where it is blowing (v. 8). So unsaved people do not understand the person who is "born again." They have no such spiritual experience in their lives. Thus Nicodemus asked, "How can these things be?" (v. 9). The Lord Jesus answered, "Art thou the teacher of Israel, and knowest not these things?" (v. 10). The Lord Jesus never flattered anyone. He soberly refers

---

3:1. Nicodemus ("Conqueror over the people") was a member of the Sanhedrin, the ruling body of elders over the Jews. Here he came secretly by night, but at the end he came bringing a hundred pounds of spices, a gift fit for a King (19:39). See *ZPEB*, "Nicodemus," IV, pp. 434–35; *ISBE*, "Nicodemus," III, p. 533; Harrison, R. K., ed., *The New Unger's Bible Dictionary*, "Nicodemus," p. 921.

3:3. Regeneration refers to a spiritual birth of life from God that transforms the individual into a child of God. See *ZPEB*, "Regeneration," V, pp. 52–57; *ISBE*, "Regeneration," IV, pp. 67–71; *EDBT*, "New Birth," pp. 558–59; *NDBT*, "Regeneration," pp. 720–23; Berkhof, L., *Systematic Theology*, "Regeneration," pp. 465–76.

The kingdom of God is the sphere of God's rule. He rules over all that exists, but in a more specific sense He rules the lives and actions of good men and angels. There is a limiting action in His rule over evil angels and wicked men. All will ultimately be brought to account. For discussion see *ZPEB*, "Kingdom of God, of Heaven," III, pp. 801–809; *ISBE*, "Kingdom of God," III, pp. 23–29; *EDBT*, "Kingdom of God," pp. 451–54; and from a liberal perspective, see John Bright, *The Kingdom of God*.

3:3–8. Being *born again* refers to the doctrine of regeneration. See v. 3 note. The unsaved person is spiritually dead (Rom. 6:13). The Spirit of God must impart new life to the believer to make him a child of God (John 3:5–8). There is no physical explanation for the action of the Spirit of God. The believer is a new creation in Christ (II Cor. 5:17).

to Nicodemus as the outstanding teacher of Israel. The Lord said, "Amen, amen, I say to you that we are speaking that which we know, and we are testifying that which we have seen, and you are not receiving our testimony" (v. 11). The Lord went on to say, "If I have told you [plural] earthly things, and ye believe not, how shall ye believe, if I tell you of heavenly things?" (v. 12). The Jews had no spiritual perception to understand the truth.

The Lord continued, "No man has ascended up to heaven, but he that came down from heaven" (v. 13*a*). The Lord Jesus alone had the power to come to earth or to return to heaven. But He had come to earth for a very definite purpose: "The Son of man must be lifted up, that whosoever believeth in him should not perish, but have eternal life" (3:14*b*–15). He came to provide salvation for everyone who would believe in Him. The Lord Jesus mentioned that Moses lifted up the serpent of brass in the wilderness so that the people who had been bitten by the fiery snakes would be healed by the power of Jehovah (authenticating Num. 21:6–9). This may be a reference to the reddish-colored carpet viper (See Azaria Alon, *The Natural History of the Land of the Bible*, color plate, p. 203). So the Lord Jesus must be lifted up on the cross so that all who look upon Him might be redeemed by His saving power. Now the Lord speaks the most famous verse in all the Bible. "For God so loved the world, that he gave his only begotten Son, that whosoever believeth in him should not perish, but have everlasting life" (3:16). This is the verse that has led more people to the Lord Jesus Christ as Savior than any other. It is the gospel message in a single sentence. God

---

3:10. The Lord's use of the article ("*the* teacher of Israel") singles out Nicodemus.

3:14. The reference is to the serpent of brass lifted up on a pole (Num. 21:8–9). It is the only time that *serpent* is mentioned in John.

3:16. This verse is the fulfillment of Isa. 9:6. It is a powerful declaration of the infinite love of God. It is the single verse that is best known, and perhaps most influential in bringing people to saving faith in the Lord Jesus Christ. John is the apostle of love. He uses the verb *to love* (*agapao*) 37 times: John 3:16, 19, 35; 8:42; 10:17; 11:5; 12:43; 13:1 [2], 23, 34 [3]; 14:15, 21 [4], 23 [2], 24, 28, 31; 15:9 [2], 12 [2], 17; 17:23 [2]; 24, 26; 19:26; 21:7, 15, 16, 20. For the noun see John 5:42 note. For *love* see *ZPEB*, "Love," III, pp. 989–96; *ISBE*, "Love," III, pp. 173–76; *EDBT*, "Love," pp. 494–95; *NDBT*, "Love," pp. 646–50.

Muslims will say that God could not have a Son because they are thinking of a literal biological offspring of the Father and Mary. They fail to see that Scripture is referring to "the intimate spiritual relationship between God and Jesus" (*The Apologetics Study Bible*, p. 1575).

did not send His Son into the world to judge the world, but that the world might be saved through Him (v. 17). Thus verse 17 is an explanation of verse 16. The Lord Jesus died upon the cross as a vicarious, substitutionary sacrifice for the sins of the world. Whoever will not believe in Him stands condemned (v. 18). People still turn away into darkness to hide their sins, rather than coming to Christ for His forgiveness (v. 19). Evildoers still hate the light and avoid it (v. 20). But in contrast people who do the truth come to the light that their deeds may be made manifest, that they are wrought in God (v. 21). *Doing the truth* means living their lives in obedience to God's will, revealed in His Word. Their deeds are worked, performed, in the power of God.

II. John the Baptist Testifies to Christ. vv. 22–30.

After these things Jesus came into the land of Judea and was baptizing His followers (v. 22). John the Baptist was near by at Aenon near Salim (v. 23). The location of Aenon is uncertain (see *ZPEB*, "Aenon," I, pp. 66–67; *ISBE*, "Aenon," I, p. 60). It was on the west side of Jordan. John was not yet cast into prison (v. 24). A question arose between John's disciples and the Jews about purification (v. 25). His disciples came to John and mentioned the success of the Lord Jesus in baptizing followers (v. 26). John wisely replied that a man can receive nothing except God gives it (v. 27). He was never jealous over the success of the Lord Jesus in preaching. He understood that he was only a forerunner (v. 28). John went on to identify himself as the friend of the Bridegroom, not the Bridegroom Himself (v. 29). John went on to declare a maxim for all Christian workers: "He must increase, but I must decrease" (v. 30). John understood that God's will for him was imprisonment and martyrdom. The Lord Jesus Christ would accomplish all the salvation of God's people. No one could help Him. All Christian workers need to recognize that Christ is the One Who enables all Christian workers to accomplish God's will. Without Him, we can do nothing (15:5).

3:20. The verb *to hate* occurs 12 times in John (3:20; 7:7; 12:25; 15:18, 19, 23, 24, 25; 17:14).

3:21. The idea of "doing the truth" is living out the truths of God's Word. It is not enough to know what God's Word teaches. The believer must "live out" the teaching of Scripture in his daily practice. See also Matt. 7:24–25. Compare John 17:17.

3:29. Joy is mentioned 9 times in John (3:29; 15:11 [2]; 16:20–24; 17:13). See *ZPEB*, "Joy," III, pp. 714–15; *ISBE*, "Joy," II, pp. 1140–42.

III. John the Apostle Explains the Greatness of Christ. vv. 31–36.

John understood the divine nature of Christ: "He that cometh from above" and "He whom God hath sent" (vv. 31, 34) clearly refer to the preexistent Christ as the divine Son. The Holy Spirit rests upon Him in all His fullness (v. 34). The Father has delegated to the Son all authority (v. 35). To believe on the Son brings everlasting life; to refuse to believe in Him brings the abiding wrath of God (v. 36). This is the only time that this word for the divine wrath of God is mentioned in John's Gospel. The person who receives the testimony concerning the Lord Jesus Christ has set His seal to the fact that "God is true" (v. 33).

Practical Applications from John 3

1. Nicodemus is not the only man to come to Jesus secretly, fearing the disapproval of the world (v. 2).
2. The Lord Jesus did not waste any time. He immediately brought up the need of the new birth (v. 3).
3. Nicodemus did not understand spiritual things. The Lord explained them to him with great care (vv. 5ff.).
4. The Lord used the Old Testament to illustrate the new teaching (v. 14).
5. The Lord emphasized God's great love (v. 16).
6. The Lord warned that the unbeliever stands condemned already (v. 18).
7. Men perversely love darkness rather than the light (v. 19).
8. One who practices the truth comes to the light (v. 21).
9. John was not disturbed by the Lord's success (v. 27).

3:35–36. God the Father loves the Son and has made the salvation of all people depend on the person's faith in the divine Son, Jesus Christ.

3:36. The wrath of God is God's righteous anger against sin and evil. It is mentioned only here in John. See Matt. 3:7; Rom. 1:18; 2:5; 5:9; 9:22; Eph. 2:3; 5:6; Col. 3:6; I Thess. 1:10; 2:16; 5:9; Heb. 3:11; 4:3; Rev. 6:16, 17; 11:18; 16:19; 19:15. See *ZPEB*, "Wrath," V, pp. 990–95; *ISBE*, "Wrath," IV, pp. 1134–35; *EDBT*, "Wrath of God," pp. 845–46; *NDBT*, "Anger," pp. 381–83; Tasker, R. V. G., *The Biblical Doctrine of the Wrath of God*.

10. The Christian principle is always "He must increase, but I must decrease" (v. 30).
11. The only alternative to the love of God is the wrath of God (v. 36).

Prayer
Dear Lord, enable us to proclaim Your Word so that men might come to believe that You are the only begotten Son of God. We pray in Your name. Amen.

JOHN 4

Jesus and the Samaritan Woman

Persons

Jesus
His disciples
Jacob
Joseph
a woman of Samaria
God
the Savior of the world
a certain nobleman
his son
his servants

Persons mentioned

the Pharisees
John the Baptist
Jews
Jacob
Joseph
Samaritans
five husbands
one who is not a husband
God the Father
the fathers
true worshippers
Messiah
men of the city

Places mentioned

Judea
Galilee
Samaria
Sychar
Jerusalem
Cana
Capernaum

Doctrines taught

baptism
living water
everlasting life
worship
God is a Spirit
salvation
soul winning
God
Messiah
believe
miracles

John 4 Exposition

I. Jesus Rescues the Samaritan Woman. vv. 1–26.

The Lord Jesus left Judea and went through Samaria towards Galilee. He came to the well at Sychar and sat on the stone seat there (vv. 5–6). Jacob's well is still there. A woman of Samaria came to draw water at midday, which was unusual in the heat. Jesus asked her, "Give me to drink" (v. 7). The disciples had gone into the city to buy food (v. 8). The Samaritan woman asked the Lord, "How is it that thou, being a Jew, askest drink of me, a woman of Samaria?" She is thinking that He must be awfully thirsty! But the Lord answered, "If thou knewest the gift of God, and who it is that saith to thee, Give me to drink; thou wouldest have asked of him, and he would have given thee living water" (v. 10). The woman rises to the bait and twits Him about having no pitcher to fill with water (v. 11). Now she asks, "Art thou greater than our father Jacob, who gave us the well?" (v. 12). The Samaritans claimed descent from Jacob through Ephraim and Manasseh. The Lord then says, "The water that I shall give him shall be in him a well of water springing up into everlasting life" (v. 14). Now the woman begs for some of this water: "Lord, give me this water, that I thirst not" (v. 15*a*). The Lord now causes the woman to face her sin: "Go, call thy

---

4:1–3. The Lord knew that the Pharisees had heard of His popular preaching.

4:2. Why did Jesus not baptize converts? It would be a temptation to pride in the later church. See I Cor. 1:14–17.

4:4. For background see *ISBE*, "Samaria, Country of," IV, pp. 298–303; *ZPEB*, "Samaria, Territory of," V, pp. 240–43; McRay, John, *Archaeology and the New Testament*, pp. 145–48.

4:5. Where was Sychar? It was a small city close to Shechem. It was the traditional site of Jacob's well, which is still pointed out there. The modern village is called Balatah. See *ISBE*, "Sychar," IV, pp. 674–75; "Shechem," IV, pp. 458–62; *ZPEB*, "Sychar," V, pp. 549–50; McRay, John, *Archaeology and the New Testament*, Sychar, pp. 179–83.

4:6–7. The woman deliberately came about noon, when she knew that other women would be at home fixing lunch. She had met barbed tongues before.

4:9. Why was the woman surprised that Jesus asked for water? In the prejudices of that day, a Jew would rather have died of thirst than ask a Samaritan for anything. Water was not only an agent of cleansing but also one of sustaining life. See *ISBE*, "Water," IV, pp. 1024–26; *ZPEB*, "Water," V., pp. 902–6.

4:11. The word *Lord, Sir* (*kurie*) is used as an address 34 times in John (4:11, 15, 19, 49; 5:7; 6:34, 68; 8:11; 9:36, 38; 11:3, 12, 21, 27, 32, 34, 39, etc).

4:14. What was the meaning of "the water that I shall give him"? The Lord was referring to the salvation symbolized by the washing of water. "The fear of the Lord is a fountain of life, to depart from the snares of death" (Prov. 14:27). See *ISBE*, "Salvation," IV, pp. 287–95.

husband." She tries to brazen it away: "I have no husband." But the Lord replies, "Thou hast well said, I have no husband: for thou hast had five husbands; and he whom thou now hast is not thy husband: in that saidst thou truly" (vv. 17–18). The woman now says, "Lord, I perceive that thou art a prophet." And now she tries to turn the conversation into a theological question: where is the proper place of worship (v. 20)? The Lord pierces through all this and declares, "Woman, believe me, the hour cometh, when ye shall neither in this mountain, nor yet at Jerusalem, worship the Father. Ye worship ye know not what: we know what we worship: for salvation is of the Jews" (vv. 21–22). They had the inspired texts of the Old Testament; the Messiah comes from the Jews. "God is a Spirit: and they that worship him must worship him in spirit and in truth" (v. 24). The woman expressed a Messianic hope, and the Lord claimed point-blank "I that speak unto thee am he" (vv. 25–26).

II. Jesus Ministers to the Samaritans. vv. 27–45.

The disciples marveled that He talked with a woman, which was contrary to custom. The woman did some clever advertising. She spoke to the men about a man "who told me all things that ever I did; this cannot be the messiah [can it?]" (v. 29). By expressing doubt the woman stirred their curiosity. The men went out to see for themselves and came to faith in Christ (v. 42). The disciples urged the Lord to eat something, but He said, "I have food to eat that ye know not of" (v. 32). The disciples wondered who had brought Him food (v. 33). Jesus said, "My food is to do the will of him that sent me, and to finish his work" (v. 34).

4:18. "Thou hast had five husbands" is evidence of the Lord's divine omniscience. The woman recognizes that He has prophetic gifts.

4:20–24. The word *worship* occurs 9 times in this context (4:20–24) and only twice elsewhere in John (9:38; 12:20).

4:24. "God is a Spirit." As Spirit He is "absolutely free from all limitations of space and time" (Westcott, p. 73). The ultimate reality is the personality of God. *ZPEB*, "God," II, pp. 742–58; V, pp. 503f.; *ISBE*, "God," II, pp. 493–503; "Spirit," IV, pp. 599–601; *EDBT*, "God," pp. 288–95; *NDBT*, "God," pp. 511–21; Bavinck, Herman, *The Doctrine of God*, 407 pp.

4:25. It is significant that the Messianic hope was not limited to Jews alone. *ZPEB*, "Messiah," IV, pp. 198–207; *ISBE*, "Messiah," III, pp. 330–38; *EDBT*, "Messiah," pp. 523–25. Compare I Thess. 4:13–18.

4:34. The great purpose of the Lord Jesus Christ was to do the will of His heavenly Father. See *ISBE*, "Will of God," IV, pp. 1064–67; *EDBT*, "Will of God," pp. 820–22.

The Samaritans besought Him to tarry with them, and for two days He stayed and ministered to them. Many of them believed and found out that He was the "Savior of the world," not just of Jews (v. 42). After two days, He went on to Galilee (v. 43). When He came to Galilee, the Galileans received Him, having seen the miracles He did at the feast (v. 45).

III. Jesus Heals the Nobleman's Son. vv. 46–54.

When Jesus came again to Cana of Galilee, a nobleman (literally "a petty king") begged the Lord to come and heal his son, who was at the point of death (vv. 46–47). The Lord Jesus said, "Except ye see signs and wonders, ye will not believe" (v. 48). But the nobleman begged Him, "Lord, come down ere my child die" (v. 49). Jesus commanded him, "Go thy way; thy son lives." The man believed and went home. His servants met him and gave him the good news, "Thy son lives" (v. 51). He asked when his son had begun to amend, and he found that it was the very hour that Jesus had spoken the word of healing (v. 53). He and his whole household became believers. This was the second miracle that Jesus had done when He came from Judea to Galilee (v. 54).

Practical Applications from John 4

1. The Lord Jesus struck up a conversation with a total stranger (vv. 7ff.). So did Paul (Acts 17:17).
2. The Lord led the conversation to God and His gift of salvation (vv. 10–21). So did Paul (Acts 16:13).
3. Many people think that they worship God, but they are not worshiping the God of the Bible (v. 22).
4. The woman went on to deliberately provoke interest in Christ (vv. 28–30). The result was that many came to believe in Him (vv. 39–40).

4:35. "The fields white unto harvest" refer to the people all around them who needed Christ. We are all in the same situation.

4:36–38. The verb *to reap* occurs only in these verses in John.

4:42. The Samaritans had heard the Lord for themselves and knew that He was the Savior of the world, not just of Jews.

4:49. The nobleman addressed the Lord Jesus literally as "Lord." The Lord Jesus responded at once.

4:54. Literally this was the second *sign* that Jesus did. See John 2:11 note.

5. The Samaritans found out that Jesus Christ was not just the Savior of the Jews, but of the whole world of mankind (v. 42).
6. All the Gospels record that Jesus said, "a prophet hath no honour in his own country" (4:44; Matt. 13:57; Mark 6:4; Luke 4:24). It is a widely known truism.
7. Jesus healed the son of the nobleman, and as a result his whole household was saved (vv. 47–54).

Prayer

Dear Lord, help us to worship You in spirit and in truth. Give us a sense of Your presence with us in prayer. For Jesus' sake. Amen.

JOHN 5

Healing at Bethesda and Teaching on the Father

Persons

the Lord Jesus
the Jews
impotent people
the man impotent for 38 years
the Jews
God the Father
the dead

Persons mentioned

an angel
all that are in the graves
John the Baptist
Moses

Places mentioned

Jerusalem
pool of Bethesda
the temple

Doctrines taught

the Sabbath
the resurrection of life
the resurrection of condemnation
judgment
the necessity of searching the Scriptures
eternal life
the love of God
faith in Christ

John 5 Exposition

I. Healing at the Pool of Bethesda. vv. 1–18.

5:2. The pool at the sheep market is a long one, having a colonnade on each of the four sides, and one across the middle. This would provide some shade for the people who came for water. The foundations of the pillars can still be seen. There was a man there who had been afflicted with an infirmity for 38 years. The Lord Jesus asked him if he wanted to be made whole (v. 6). He complained that he had no one to help him get into the water (v. 7). The Lord Jesus commanded him, "Rise, take up thy bed, and walk" (v. 8). The man was immediately made whole and walked (v. 8). When the man found out that it was Jesus Who had made him whole, he told the authorities, and they sought to slay Jesus because He had done the healing on the Sabbath (vv. 15–16). To them a great miracle was nothing; the letter of the law was everything. The Lord Jesus said, "My Father works hitherto, and I work" (v. 17). Now the authorities sought the more to kill Jesus because He claimed that God was His Father, "making himself equal with God" (v. 18). Unsaved people do not understand the divine unity of the Trinity. There is no competition between the Persons. The Lord Jesus Christ does the will of His Father perfectly.

5:2. For discussion on the pool of Bethesda see *ISBE*, "Bethesda," I, pp. 467–68; *ZPEB*, "Beth-Zatha," I, pp. 549–51; McRay, John, *Archeology and the New Testament*, "the Pool of Bethesda," pp. 186–88. See Custer, *Stones of Witness*, pp. 108, 120, for color photographs. For a porter carrying a refrigerator on his back see p. 113. The author remembers seeing a lady walk away from a pool with a 50-gallon drum balanced on her head.

5:4. The tradition was that an angel periodically troubled the waters, and the first person in the waters afterwards was healed. The Lord Jesus had the power to heal without any means.

5:8. The Lord Jesus commanded the man to do what he could not do, and the man, seeking to obey, was healed in the process by the power of the Lord.

5:14. The Lord Jesus commanded the man to "stop keeping on sinning" (Pres. tense), lest something worse come upon him.

5:18. The language is conclusive. The Jews were seeking to kill Jesus, "not only because he was breaking the Sabbath, but also because he was saying that God was his very own Father, making himself equal to God."

II. Teaching on the Son and the Father. vv. 19–47.

The Son is doing the things that the Father desires (v. 19). As the Father raises the dead, even so the Son will raise the dead (v. 21). The Father has committed all judgment to the Son, that all should honor the Son, even as they honor the Father (vv. 22–23). The Lord gave a clear promise: "He that heareth my word, and believeth on him that sent me, hath everlasting life, and shall not come into condemnation; but is passed from death unto life" (v. 24). The Lord said, "Truly, truly, I say unto you, The hour is coming, and now is, when the dead shall hear the voice of the Son of God: and they that hear shall live" (v. 25). As the Father has life in Himself, so He has granted that the Son have life in Himself (v. 26). He has also granted the Son to have authority to execute judgment (v. 27). The time is coming when the Son will raise the righteous dead in a resurrection of life, and the wicked in a resurrection of condemnation (v. 29). The Lord prophesied that the dead "shall come forth; they that have done good, unto the resurrection of life; and they that have done evil, unto the resurrection of condemnation" (v. 29). The Lord also claimed that "my judgment is just; because I seek not mine own will, but the will of the Father who has sent me" (v. 30). He reminded them that John the Baptist had witnessed to Him (v. 33). The Lord Jesus was teaching them that they might be saved (v. 34), but they would not listen. The Lord commends John the Baptist as a burning and shining light (v. 35). But the works of Jesus are a greater witness than John (v. 36). The Father Himself has borne witness at the baptism (v. 37; Matt. 3:14–17). Now the Lord gives a timeless command: "Continue searching

---

5:19. The Lord Jesus refers to Himself as "the Son" on numerous occasions. See also John 5:20, 21, 22, 23, 26; 6:40; 8:35, 36; 14:13. See also Matt. 11:27; Luke 10:22.

5:25. What is the meaning of this statement? "The hour . . . now is, when the [spiritually] dead shall hear the voice of the Son of God and . . . shall live." Contrast John 5:28–29*a*: "The hour is coming, in which all that are in the graves shall hear his voice, and shall come forth."

5:33–39. There is a fourfold witness to Christ recorded here:

John the Baptist witnessed to Christ (5:33–35).

The works of Christ witness to Him (5:36).

The Father has borne witness to Christ (5:37–38).

The Scriptures testify to Christ (5:39). See also *ISBE*, "Messiah," III, pp. 330–38; *ZPEB*, "Messiah," IV, pp. 198–207.

the Scriptures" (v. 39). He testified, "They are they which testify of me." The continuing study of the Holy Scriptures is the believer's responsibility. Every believer should be a diligent student of the Bible. God guides His people through His Word. To turn away from the Scriptures is to stumble into spiritual darkness. Coming in faith to the Lord Jesus gives eternal life (v. 40). Men should seek the honor that comes from God only (v. 44). Moses condemned the wicked (v. 45). He also wrote of the future Messiah (v. 46, Gen. 3:15; 22:18; 49:10). The Lord challenged the audience, "But if ye believe not his writings, how shall ye believe my words?" (v. 47). The Lord Jesus warned on another occasion, "The scripture cannot be broken" (10:35*b*). The Bible is a much more powerful Book than unbelievers realize.

Practical Applications from John 5

1. The solution for man's problems is not following vain superstitions, but coming to the Lord Jesus Christ (vv. 7–9).
2. The main objection to Jesus was that He is equal to God the Father (v. 18).
3. The Father has committed all judgment to the Son; all must answer to Him (v. 22, 27). See *ZPEB*, "Judging, Judgment," III, pp. 758–60; *ISBE*, "Judging, Judge," II, pp. 1161–62.
4. The obligation of all men is to keep on searching the Scriptures (v. 39). See II Tim. 3:16; II Pet. 1:19–21.
5. Coming to the Lord Jesus Christ imparts eternal life to the believer (v. 40).

5:39. The Lord uses a present-tense imperative verb, "Continue searching the Scriptures." All men have a continuing responsibility of searching the Scriptures in order to ascertain the will of God and the plan of His salvation. There are many people who read the Bible as a good religious book, but finding Christ in Scripture is the most important element of Bible study. For an exhaustive example see Hengstenberg, *The Christology of the Old Testament*, 4 vols. See also Edersheim, *The Life of Jesus the Messiah*, 2 vols.

5:42. The noun *love* (*agape*) occurs 7 times in John 5:42; 13:35; 15:9, 10 [2], 13; 17:26. For the verb see John 3:16 note.

5:46. Note the Lord's authorization of Messianic prophecy. Moses wrote of Him (Gen. 3:15; Deut. 18:15). See also II Sam. 7:12–13; Ps. 2:6–12; Ps. 22; Isa. 53; Jer. 23:5–6; Mic. 5:2; Dan. 7:13–14; 9:20–27. There is a bond of divine inspiration that binds biblical prophecy together.

6. The main danger is looking for honor from men, rather than from God alone (v. 44). See Ps. 56:4; Prov. 29:25.
7. If one does not read the Old Testament, he is repudiating part of God's Holy Word (vv. 46–47).

Prayer

Dear Lord, protect us from seeking honor from men instead of from You. Enable us to exalt the Scriptures in our lives and to continue searching them for Your truth. Amen.

JOHN 6

The Feeding of the Five Thousand

Persons

Jesus
a great multitude
5000 men
His disciples
Philip
Andrew
Simon Peter
God the Father
the Living Father
the Living God
the Son

Persons mentioned

a lad
that prophet that should come
a king
the prophets
I am the living bread
I am the bread of life
the Son of man
disciples
Joseph
the Jews
your fathers
the Spirit
Judas Iscariot
many of His disciples (who walked no more with Him)
the Twelve

Places mentioned

Sea of Galilee
Tiberias
a mountain
Capernaum
the desert
the world
Heaven

Doctrines taught

to give thanks for food
Jesus' miraculous power
the necessity of believing in Jesus
Jesus will raise the dead
the ascension of Jesus
The words of Jesus are spirit and life
eternal life

John 6 Exposition

I. Feeding the Five Thousand. vv. 1–21.

The Lord Jesus crossed the Sea of Galilee to the eastern side and went up into a mountain (6:1–3). A great multitude followed because they had seen His miracles of healing (v. 2). The Lord asked Philip, "Whence shall we buy bread, that these may eat?" (v. 5). Philip responded that they had nothing like enough money to do that (v. 7). Andrew mentioned that there was a lad who had five barley loaves and two small fishes, and added, "But what are they among so many?" (v. 9). There were about five thousand men (v. 10). The Lord commanded them to sit down. The place had much grass. (It was springtime.) The Lord took the loaves and when He had given thanks, He was giving to the ones who were reclining, and of the fishes as much as they were wishing (v. 11, lit.). When they all had eaten, the Lord commanded to gather up the fragments that remained, and they filled twelve baskets with the fragments (v. 13).

When the men realized the miracle that had occurred, they said, "This is truly the prophet that is coming into the world" (v. 14). When Jesus perceived that they would come and force Him to be a king, He departed into a mountain alone (v. 15). When evening came, His disciples went down and boarded a ship and went toward Capernaum. It was dark and Jesus had not come (v. 17). A storm arose, and the wind was against them (v. 18). When they had rowed 2 or 3 miles, they see Jesus walking on the sea,

---

6:1, 23. Tiberias was a city on the western shore of the Sea of Galilee. It had been founded by Herod Antipas. See *ZPEB*, "Tiberias," V, pp. 745–46; *ISBE*, "Tiberias," IV, pp. 846–47; McRay, John, *Archaeology and the New Testament*, p. 178.

6:4. For the Passover see John 2:14 note.

6:5–58. The word *bread* occurs 21 times in this chapter, and only in 13:18; 21:9, 13 elsewhere in John. See *ZPEB*, "Bread," I, pp. 648–51; *ISBE*, "Bread," I, pp. 540–44.

6:7. What was "two hundred pennyworth"? It was 200 days wages (denarii).

6:9. Barley was the food of the poor. It was a coarser grain than wheat. See *ZPEB*, "Barley," I, p. 475; *ISBE*, "Barley," I, p. 431.

6:9–11. The lad did not have much, but he gave it all to Jesus. The Lord used it to feed 5,000 people. That fact must not be lost on us.

6:17. For Capernaum see John 2:12 note.

6:19. "They see Jesus walking on the sea"—This is a clear testimony to the supernatural powers of the Lord Jesus Christ. See *ZPEB*, "Miracles," IV, pp. 241–50; *ISBE*, "Miracle," III, pp. 371–81; *EDBT*, "Miracle," pp. 531–34.

drawing near them (v. 19). They were afraid, but He called to them, "It is I; be not afraid" (v. 20). They gladly received Him into the ship, "and immediately the ship was at the land whither they went" (v. 21). Thus the Lord showed His disciples His total control over the weather, circumstances, and the deeds of men.

II. Christ the Bread of Life. vv. 22–71.

When the people saw that Jesus and His disciples were gone, they also took boats and crossed the Sea of Galilee and came to Capernaum (vv. 22–24). They ask Him, "Rabbi, when camest thou hither?" (v. 25). The Lord Jesus reproached them for following Him just because He had fed them with the miraculous loaves (vv. 26–27). They should be seeking Him for everlasting life, not just food. When they ask Him how to work the works of God, He answers, "This is the work of God, that ye believe on him whom he hath sent" (v. 29). When they ask for a sign from Him, and suggest manna from heaven, He said, "My Father giveth you the true bread from heaven. For the bread of God is he which cometh down from heaven, and giveth life unto the world " (vv. 32–33). They quickly ask, "Lord, evermore give us this bread" (v. 34). Jesus then declares, "I am the bread of life: he that cometh

---

6:21. The presence of the Lord Jesus Christ is the solution for every problem and danger for the believer.

6:31. For *manna* see *ZPEB*, "Manna," IV, p. 68; *ISBE*, "Manna," III, pp. 239–40.

6:35. Jesus' claim, "I am the Bread of life," means that He is the One Who sustains His people. See also John 6:48–51. Bread was the staff of life in the ancient world. See Robinson, William Childs, *Christ—the Bread of Life*, 190 pp.; Westcott, B. F., *John*, p. 102; Godet, F., *John*, vol. II, pp. 22–23; Borchert, Gerald, *John 1–11*, pp. 264–65; *EDBT*, "Bread," pp. 75–76.

For the "I am" claims of the Lord Jesus see:

1. I am the Bread of life. John 6:35, 48.
2. I am the Light of the world. John 8:12.
3. I am the Door. John 10:7, 9.
4. I am the Good Shepherd. John 10:11, 14.
5. I am the Resurrection and the Life. John 11:25.
6. I am the Way, the Truth, and the Life. John 14:6.
7. I am the true Vine. John 15:5.

"I am" is the Absolute name of Jehovah God. John 18:5, 8. See also Exod. 3:14. See *ISBE*, "God, Names of," II, pp. 504–9; *ZPEB*, "Name," IV, pp. 360–66; *EDBT*, "Name," pp. 550–51.

to me shall never hunger; and he that believeth on me shall never thirst" (v. 35). He warns them that they have seen Him and still do not believe (v. 36). But He promises, "All that the Father giveth me shall come to me; and him that cometh to me I will in no wise cast out" (v. 37). These are life-changing promises when the believer claims them for his own. The Lord Jesus came down from heaven to do His Father's will (v. 38). The Father's will is that Jesus would lose nothing that the Father has given Him, "but should raise it up again at the last day" (v. 39*b*). The Lord Jesus declares His Father's will exactly: "And this is the will of him that sent me, that every one which seeth the Son, and believeth on him, may have everlasting life: and I will raise him up at the last day" (v. 40). The Jews murmur over this, "Is not this Jesus, the son of Joseph, whose father and mother we know? How is it then that he saith, I came down from heaven?" (v. 42). The Lord Jesus explained, "No man can come to me, except the Father which hath sent me draw him: and I will raise him up at the last day" (v. 44). The heavenly Father must draw the individual to God or he will not naturally come. The Lord goes on to claim, "He that believeth on me hath everlasting life. I am that bread of life" (vv. 47*b*–48). The manna sustained the Israelites for a time (v. 49). But the Lord goes on to claim, "I am the living bread which came down from heaven: if any man eat of this bread, he shall live for ever: and the bread that I will give is my flesh, which I will give for the life of the world" (v. 51). The Jews argued among themselves over what all this meant (v. 52). The Lord Jesus said to them, "Verily, verily, I say unto you, Except ye eat the flesh of the Son of man, and drink his blood, ye have no life in you" (v. 53). Unless there is a heartfelt reception of the Lord Jesus Christ as the divine Savior, there is no salvation. The "eating" of Christ's flesh and blood is a spiritual acceptance of Him as Savior,

---

6:38. For the will of God see John 4:34 note.

6:39. The word *last* occurs in John only in the phrase *the last day* (6:39, 40, 44, 54, 7:37; 11:24; 12:48).

6:39–40. The believer's security does not depend on how hard he can "hang on," but on the keeping power of the Lord Jesus Christ. He referred to Himself in saying, "he that eateth of this bread shall live forever" (v. 58*b*). See *ISBE*, "Secure, Security," IV, pp. 378–79.

6:44. Note the supernatural nature of Christian faith: the Father must draw the believer to Christ. A man may accept Christianity as a philosophy, but he must accept Christ as the Savior from sin, or remain lost. The believer has the promise of Christ, "I will raise him up at the last day" (v. 44*b*).

6:56. It is not physical eating that is involved, but spiritual reception.

not physical eating (vv. 53–56). "Eating Christ" is spiritually receiving Him (v. 57). The Lord Jesus is the true bread that came down from heaven (v. 58). The Lord warned people that He was going to ascend back to His Father (v. 62), and that no man is naturally saved (v. 65). Many of those people who had followed Jesus with enthusiasm "went back, and walked no more with him" (v. 66). Jesus asked the 12 apostles, "Will ye also go away?" (v. 67). Peter answered for them all, "We believe and are sure that thou art that Christ, the Son of the living God" (v. 69). But Jesus answered, "Have not I chosen you twelve, and one of you is a devil?" (v. 70). He was referring to Judas Iscariot (v. 71). The devil possessed Judas, and Judas finally went to his own place (Acts 1:25).

Practical Applications from John 6

1. Enable us to be always ready to receive You into our fellowship (v. 21).
2. Grant that we may have a single-minded purpose of pleasing You rather than ourselves or others (v. 26).
3. Deliver us from a complaining, murmuring spirit (v. 43).
4. Enable us to draw our spiritual strength from You as the Bread of life (v. 48).
5. Give us the spiritual perception to understand the words of the Lord (v. 63).

Prayer

Dear Lord, enable us to be sure that You are the Christ, the Son of the living God. Help us to serve You with all of our hearts. For Jesus' sake. Amen.

6:59. For the synagogue see *ISBE*, "Synagogue," IV, pp. 676–84; *ZPEB*, "Synagogue," V, pp. 554–67; *EDBT*, "Synagogue," pp. 752–54.

6:62. The Lord Jesus clearly prophesied His coming ascension. See also Acts 1:9–11.

6:63. The flesh (human effort) is of no spiritual value; the words of Christ are powerful instruments of the Spirit for life.

6:64. Betrayal by Judas is a clear theme in John (6:64, 71; 12:4; 13:2, 11, 21; 18:2, 5; 21:20).

6:71. For the Devil's possession of Judas see John 13:27. For further discussion of Judas see *ZPEB*, "Judas Iscariot," III, p. 732; *ISBE*, "Judas Iscariot," II, pp. 1151–53; Harrison, R. K., ed., *The New Unger's Bible Dictionary*, "Judas Iscariot," pp. 720–21. See also John 12:4; 13:2, 26, 29; 18:2, 3, 5.

JOHN 7

The Feast of Tabernacles

Persons

Jesus
the Jews
Jesus' brethren
the Pharisees
the chief priests
the people
Nicodemus

Persons mentioned

God
Moses
the rulers
officers
the Gentiles
the Holy Spirit
the Prophet (Deut. 18:15)
Christ the Messiah
David

Places mentioned

Galilee
the world
the temple
Jerusalem
Bethlehem

Doctrines taught

Moses gave the Law
the Sabbath
the Scripture
The works of the world are evil
No one keeps the law
the dispersion
Jesus is the Messiah

John 7 Exposition

I. Jesus Goes from Galilee to Jerusalem. vv. 1–13.

The Lord Jesus stayed in Galilee to avoid the assassination plots (v. 1). His brethren thought that He had to drum up support by human methods (vv. 3–5). But He understood the antipathy that the world has toward the things of God (vv. 7–8). The Lord always did things exactly on time. But He went secretly to Jerusalem for the Feast of Tabernacles (v. 10). The Jews sought Him, and there were murmurings and divisions among the people over Him (vv. 11–12). No one spoke openly of Him for fear of the authorities (v. 13).

II. Jesus Teaches in the Temple. vv. 14–39.

What is the meaning of the Jews' question "How knoweth this man letters, having never learned?" (v. 15). It does not mean that they thought that He was illiterate but that He had not been trained in the approved rabbinic schools. The Lord Jesus was teaching them the will of His heavenly Father (vv. 16ff.). He knew that will perfectly. Moses gave them the Law, but none of them were consistent in keeping the law (v. 19). The people who ask "Who goes about to kill you?" (v. 20) were probably ignorant of the plots against the Lord. He went on to argue that there were things that transcended the Sabbath in importance (vv. 22–24). Some in the audience perceived that Jesus was the one the authorities wanted to kill (v. 25). The

---

7:2. For the Feast of Tabernacles see Lev. 23:34.

7:3–5. Who were the "brethren" of the Lord? They were sons of Joseph and Mary, born after the Lord Jesus. They are named in Matt. 13:55 as James, Joses, Simon, and Judas. For discussion see *ISBE*, "Brothers of the Lord," I, pp. 551–52; *ZPEB*, "Brothers of Jesus, The," I, pp. 658–66.

7:7. The reason that the world hates Jesus is that He testifies that the world is evil. See *ISBE*, "World," IV, pp. 1112–16; *ZPEB*, "World," V, pp. 963–68; *EDBT*, "World," pp. 836–37; *NDBT*, "World," pp. 853–55.

7:17. The key to knowing scriptural doctrine is the willingness to obey whatever it teaches. To *hear* God's Word regularly means willingness to obey (Isa. 66:5). James 1:22–25 emphasizes the difference between merely hearing and the hearing that leads to obeying. See *ISBE*, "Hear; Hearken," II, pp. 649–50; *ZPEB*, "Obedience," IV, pp. 482–84; *EDBT*, "Hear, Hearing," pp. 330–31.

7:26, 32, 48. John refers to the Jewish leaders as "rulers, officers, chief priests," but never as "elders." The other Gospels refer to them as elders (Matt. 21:23; Mark 11:27; Luke 20:1). John calls himself "the Elder" (II John 1; III John 1; he had outlived all the others) and prophesied concerning the 24 elders in the celestial throne room (Rev. 4:4, 10).

Lord charged that many in the audience did know that He came from God, but they did not know God (v. 28). However, John the Baptist's words were prophetic: "He must increase, but I must decrease" (3:30). Many of the people believed and asked, "When Christ comes, will he do more miracles than these which this man hath done?" (v. 31). The Pharisees and the chief priests heard these murmurings of the people and sent officers to take Him (v. 32). The Pharisees and chief priests were officially opposed to Christ and desired to execute Him. The Lord Jesus warned the people that He was with them for only a short time (v. 33). In the last day of the feast the Lord Jesus cried out an invitation, "If any man thirst, let him come unto me, and drink. He that believeth on me, as the scripture hath said, out of his belly shall flow rivers of living water" (vv. 37–38). John commented that He was speaking of the future pouring out of the Holy Spirit on believers (v. 39). Isaiah had prophesied, "Behold, God is my salvation; I will trust, and not be afraid: for the Lord JEHOVAH is my strength and my song; he also is become my salvation. Therefore with joy shall ye draw water out of the wells of salvation" (Isa. 12:2–3).

III. Divided Opinions about the Lord Jesus. vv. 40–53.

Many thought that He was the Prophet foretold by Moses (Deut. 18:15, 18). Others said, "This is the Christ" (*Messiah*, as those in John 4:41–42 did). Others worried about His coming from Galilee because they had not heard of His birth in Bethlehem (v. 42). Thus the people were divided (v. 43). When the officers came back, they reported to the chief priests, "Never man spake like this man" (v. 46). There was power in His words beyond

---

7:29. This is an explicit claim by the Lord Jesus that He knows the heavenly Father and that the Father has sent Him with a commission. It is the same word used for the sending of the apostles (Matt. 15:24) and the sending of the Holy Spirit (I Pet. 1:12). The word *know* is *oida*, the "absolute, possessed knowledge such as God has," not *ginosko*, to know by experience. See Custer, *A Treasury of New Testament Synonyms*, pp. 106f.

7:31. The sheer number of miracles that Christ performed convinced many people of the truth of His Messianic claims. See *ISBE*, "Miracle," III, pp. 371–81; *EDBT*, "Miracle," pp. 531–34; *NDBT*, "Signs and Wonders," pp. 775–81.

7:35. This is the only time that the word *diaspora*, dispersion, is used in John.

7:39. For the Spirit compare John 14:16–17.

7:40. Who was "the Prophet" (7:40)? That was a reference to "the prophet like Moses" (Deut. 18:15).

7:50f. For Nicodemus see John 3:1ff.

anything they had ever heard. The Pharisees sneered that the people were deceived and did not know the law (vv. 47, 49). But Nicodemus spoke up and said, “Doth our law judge any man, before it hear him, and know what he doeth?” (7:51). But they brushed him off, saying, “Out of Galilee ariseth no prophet” (v. 52*b*). They were ignorant of Jesus’ birth in Bethlehem. See Matt. 2:1–15.

Practical Applications from John 7

1. The Lord Jesus always taught His Father’s doctrine (John 7:16). We must be careful to teach God’s Word, not our opinions.
2. Believers need a willing spirit to understand correct Bible doctrine (v. 17).
3. We need the spiritual thirst to come to Jesus and drink the spiritual truth that He will give (vv. 37–38).

Prayer

Dear Lord, give us the grace to endure the world’s hatred. Give us a single-minded devotion to Your Word. Enable us to seek Your approval over all others’. For Jesus’ sake. Amen.

JOHN 8

The Woman Taken in Adultery

Persons

the Lord Jesus
all the people
scribes
Pharisees
a woman taken in adultery
the Father
the Son of man

Persons mentioned

Moses
the Jews who believed
Abraham
the Devil
a Samaritan
the prophets
"I am" (the name of God, Exod. 3:14)

Places mentioned

Mount of Olives
the temple
the treasury

Doctrines taught

the law of Moses
Jesus the Light of the world
He that follows Me shall have the light of life
If you believe not that "I am," you shall die in your sins (8:24)
If you continue in My word, you are My disciples (8:31)
Jesus: "Before Abraham was, I am" (8:58)
the necessity of faith
The truth shall make you free
Sinners have the Devil as father

John 8 Exposition

I. The Woman Taken in Adultery. vv. 1–11.

Jesus went to the Mount of Olives, and in the morning came again to the temple and taught the people (vv. 1–2). He was systematically reaching people with His words. But the scribes and Pharisees bring a woman taken in adultery. They declare that Moses had commanded that such should be stoned (which was correct, Lev. 20:10; Deut. 22:22). They challenge Jesus to say something different (v. 5). Jesus stooped down and with His finger wrote on the ground. What did He write? It could have been the besetting sins of her accusers (v. 9). Whatever it was, they were afraid to say anything more and slipped away. Jesus asked her, "Did no one condemn you?" (v. 10). She answered, "No one, Lord." Jesus responded, "Neither do I condemn you; go and stop sinning" (v. 11). The darkness could be cleansed, but her life of habitual sin must stop. The believer must not have a divided loyalty.

II. Jesus the Light of the World. vv. 12–59.

This is one of John's great themes. "God is light, and no darkness at all is in him" (I John 1:5*b*). It was also David's theme: "The Lord is my light and my salvation; whom shall I fear?" (Ps. 27:1). Isaiah also proclaimed this truth: "The Lord shall be thine everlasting light" (Isa. 60:20*b*). The Lord Jesus could proclaim this because He knew that He came from God the Father and would return (8:14). The Lord had the Presence of the heavenly Father

---

8:1–11. There is probably no paragraph in John's Gospel more characteristic of the Lord Jesus than this one. The manuscript evidence for it is late, however. Some have thought that it was left out lest it encourage adultery. But the Scriptures deal with such sins very candidly (Ps. 51). Christ sanctifies and cleanses the church by the washing of water by the Word (Eph. 5:26–27). In the same way Christ restored this guilty woman. No one should use this account as an excuse for sin.

8:8–9. The scribes and Pharisees may have heard of the Lord's supernatural knowledge on other occasions (4:11–18). They went out one by one as they realized that others could accuse them of sins of the past.

8:11. The Lord Jesus does not encourage sin, but He does forgive sinners.

8:12. The statement of Jesus, "I am the light of the world" was prophesied by Isaiah: "The people that walked in darkness have seen a great light: they that dwell in the land of the shadow of death, upon them hath the light shined" (Isa. 9:2). For the whole series of "I am" titles see John 6:35 note. See also *ISBE*, "God, Names of," II, pp. 504–9; "Light," III, pp. 134–36; *ZPEB*, "Light," III, pp. 932–34; *EDBT*, "Light," pp. 486–87; *NDBT*, "Light," pp. 644–46.

with Him (v. 16). The unbelieving Jews ask, "Where is thy Father?" (v. 19). The Lord responded, "Ye neither know me, nor my Father" (v. 19*b*). The Lord warned them, "Ye shall seek me, and shall die in your sins: whither I go, ye cannot come" (v. 21). The Jews did not understand Him at all and thought He spoke of suicide instead of the Presence of His heavenly Father (v. 22). The Lord warned them, "Ye are from beneath; I am from above" (v. 23). They belonged to the Devil; He was one with the Father. They did not believe Him, so they were going to die in their sins (v. 24). He went on to say, "He that sent me is true" (v. 26), but they did not understand that He spoke of God the Father (v. 27). Jesus could say, "I do always those things that please him" (the Father, v. 29). Even believers can remember many times in which they have not pleased the heavenly Father. Many who heard this message did believe on Him (v. 30). Jesus said to those who believed on Him, "If ye continue in my word, then are ye my disciples indeed; and ye shall know the truth, and the truth shall make you free" (vv. 31–32). But unbelieving Jews cried out, "We are Abraham's seed, and have never been in bondage to anyone" (v. 33). But Jesus warned, "Every one who keeps on doing sin is a slave of sin" (v. 34). "The slave does not remain in the house forever; the Son remains forever" (v. 35). "If the Son shall make you free, you shall be free for ever" (v. 36). The Lord went on to say, "I know that you are Abraham's seed, but you seek to kill me, because my word has no room in you" (v. 37). They were dominated by their father,

---

8:20. Jesus was teaching in the treasury, that part of the temple area that was most open. The women also could come to that part of the temple.

8:24. If a person does not believe that Jesus is the "I am," the God Who can forgive sins, he will die in his sins. There is no other source for forgiveness. See *ZPEB*, "God, Names of," II, pp. 760–66; "Forgiveness," II, pp. 596–600; *ISBE*, "God, Names of," II, pp. 504–9; "Forgiveness," II, pp. 340–44.

8:29. The word *please, pleasing* occurs only here in John's Gospel.

8:31. The Lord Jesus makes continuance in His word the great test of genuine discipleship. See also *ISBE*, "Word," IV, pp. 1101–1107; *ZPEB*, "Word, Word of the Lord," V, pp. 956–62; *EDBT*, "Word," pp. 828–31; *NDBT*, "Word," pp. 848–53.

8:33. How could the Jews boast that they had never been slaves? In point of fact they had been slaves in Egypt, Assyria, Babylon, Persia, and some were slaves to Rome. See *The Apologetics Study Bible*, p. 1588, note.

8:35–38. The Lord Jesus invited His followers to believe on Him and to worship Him. Matthew has already taught that Jesus received worship from people (Matt. 2:11; 8:2; 9:18; 14:33; 15:25; 20:20; 28:9, 17).

the Devil, but they boldly claim, "Abraham is our father" (v. 39). But they were seeking to do the work of the Devil in silencing the Lord. He charged them, "You are doing the deeds of your father" (v. 41), obviously referring to the Devil. He went on to say, "If God were your father, you would love me, for I came forth from God" (v. 42). Now He charges them, "You are of your father the devil, and the lusts of your father you are wishing to keep doing" (v. 44*a*). "The devil is a liar and the father of it" (v. 44*b*). The Lord asks, "Which of you is convicting me of sin?" Obviously, no one has. "If I am speaking the truth, why are you not believing me?" (v. 46). "He that is of God keeps on hearing God's word [with submission]" (v. 47). "On account of this you are not hearing them, because you are not of God" (v. 47*b*). The Jews sneer at Him, "Say we not well that thou art a Samaritan, and hast a demon" (v. 48). The Lord responds, "I have not a demon, but I honor my Father, and you dishonor me" (v. 49). But He goes on to promise, "If anyone keeps my saying, he shall never taste death" (v. 51*b*). But Abraham and the prophets died. The Jews ask, "Whom makest thou thyself?" (v. 53*b*). The Lord responds, "If I honor myself, my honor is nothing: it is my Father who honors me; of whom ye say that he is your God: Yet you have not known him; but I know him" (vv. 54–55*a*). Now the Lord delivers His climaxing claim, "Truly, truly, I say to you, Before Abraham was, I AM" (v. 58). This was a clear claim to be the Jehovah God of the Old Testament. "And God said unto Moses, I AM THAT I AM: and he said, Thus shalt thou say unto the children of Israel, I AM hath sent me unto you" (Exod. 3:14). The Jews understood exactly and took up stones to cast at Him: "But Jesus hid himself and went out of the temple, going through the midst of them, and so passed by" (v. 59). They could not recognize Him unless God willed it.

8:44. The Devil, Satan, is that fallen angel who tempted Adam and Eve in the Garden as the Serpent (Gen. 3:1–14) and who brought trials upon Job to draw him away from God (Job 1:6–12). Here the Lord Jesus charges the unbelieving Jews with being children of the Devil, wicked people who follow the Devil. See also John 13:27 note and Matt. 4:1 note (*Gospel of the King*, p. 46).

8:56. "Abraham rejoiced." Saints in glory are aware of some things that happen on earth.

8:58–59. The Jews understood that "I am" was the name of Jehovah God and thus reached for stones to cast at Him. See Exod. 3:13–14; Isa. 43:10–15.

Practical Applications from John 8

1. What was the Lord's attitude toward condemning sinners? (v. 7). He was kind and forgiving, and He convicted others who were not.
2. Believers must follow the Lord Jesus to have the light of life (v. 12).
3. Without the Lord Jesus, people will die in their sins (vv. 21, 24).
4. Jesus always did those things that pleased His Father (v. 29). What do we do that pleases the Father?
5. The person who keeps on sinning is the slave of sin (v. 34). We need to be set free by the Lord Jesus.
6. The sinner belongs to his father, the Devil (v. 44).
7. The Lord Jesus existed before Abraham did (v. 58).

Prayer

Dear Lord, help us to have a forgiving spirit and to continue walking in the light. Set us free from slavery to sin. Protect us from the lies of the Devil. For Jesus' sake. Amen.

JOHN 9

Jesus Heals the Man Born Blind

Persons

Jesus
His disciples
the blind man
the neighbors
the Pharisees
the blind man's parents

Persons mentioned

the Jews
Moses
a worshipper of God

Places mentioned

Pool of Siloam
the synagogue
this world

Doctrines taught

sin
the Sabbath
miracles
the Son of God
judgment
willful blindness
worship of Jesus (v. 38)

John 9 Exposition

I. Jesus Heals the Man Born Blind. vv. 1–12.

The disciples regarded birth defects as a divine judgment. But birth defects are opportunities for people to seek God's compassion and wisdom. The Lord viewed it very positively. The work of God should be made manifest in the blind man (v. 3). All afflictions are opportunities for mankind to seek God and find His gracious love. The works of God that the Lord referred to are works of grace and healing. In the midst of the darkness of a sin-cursed world, the Lord shone as the Light of God to those who had eyes to see. His claim, "I am the light of the world," has been proven in the lives of multitudes of believers (v. 5). See John 8:12 note. Westcott noted this title and wrote, "The character is unchangeable, but the display of the character varies with the occasion" (*John*, p. 145). The Lord anointed the eyes of the blind man with mud and told him to wash in the Pool of Siloam (vv. 6–7). He did so and received his sight. The man's neighbors asked him how he received his sight (v. 10). He explained how he had obeyed the command of the Lord Jesus to wash in the Pool of Siloam and had received his sight (v. 11). The mud had no medicinal value, but obedience to the Lord's word restored his sight.

II. The Pharisees Persecute the Man Who Was Healed. vv. 13–34.

The Pharisees ask the man how he was healed. He describes how Jesus made clay and anointed his eyes and commanded him to wash in the Pool of Siloam (v. 15). The Pharisees charge that this man is not of God because

---

9:1–2. Birth defects still raise questions. At the very least birth defects are there to show that God can provide grace and help in time of need. Man is not self-sufficient. He needs God and His grace for a multitude of reasons. See *ISBE*, "Blindness," I, pp. 525–26; *EDBT*, "Blindness," pp. 70–71.

9:5. The Lord Jesus is the fulfillment of Isa. 9:2: "The people that walked in darkness have seen a great light." For the Lord Jesus and "the Light of the world" see *ISBE*, "Light," III, pp. 134–36; *EDBT*, "Light," pp. 486–87; *ZPEB*, "Light," III, pp. 932–34; Westcott, *John*, p. 145; Ryken, Wilhoit, and Longman, *Dictionary of Biblical Imagery*, "Light," pp. 509–12.

9:7. The Pool of Siloam was the major water source for Jerusalem. It is famous for the tunnel of Hezekiah that brought the water to the city. It was not known for any healing qualities. See *ZPEB*, "Siloam," V, pp. 434–37; *ISBE*, "Siloam," IV, pp. 510–11; McRay, John, *Archaeology and the New Testament*, pp. 121–25.

9:13. For the Pharisees see John 1:24 note.

9:16. For unbelievers observance of a day was more important than a miracle.

He does not keep the Sabbath (v. 16). They ask what the blind man thinks of Jesus, and he confesses, "He is a prophet" (v. 17). They interview the man's parents, and they disown all knowledge of the situation for fear of excommunication from the synagogue (vv. 18–23). The Pharisees then call the man and command him, "Give God the praise: we know that this man is a sinner" (v. 24). The man holds on to his confession: "One thing I know, that, whereas I was blind, now I see" (v. 25). They ask him to repeat what had happened (v. 26), and the man asks, "Will you also be his disciples?" (v. 27). They pounce on that and revile him, "Thou art his disciple; but we are Moses' disciples" (v. 28). The man argues with them, "Herein is a marvelous thing, that ye know not from whence he is, and yet he hath opened mine eyes. Now we know that God heareth not sinners: but if any man be a worshipper of God, and doeth his will, him he heareth" (v. 31). He added, "If this man were not of God, he could do nothing" (v. 33). But the Pharisees were furious at this and excommunicated him from the synagogue (v. 34).

III. Jesus Receives Him. vv. 35–41.

The Lord found him and asked him, "Dost thou believe on the Son of God?" (v. 35). He responded, "Who is he, Lord, that I might believe on him?" (v. 36). The word *Lord* shows his total submission to the Lord Jesus. The man responded, "Lord, I believe," and worshipped Him (v. 38). The Lord Jesus declared, "For judgment I am come into this world, that they which see not might see; and that they which see might be made blind" (v. 39). The formerly blind man had not only his physical sight but also his spiritual perception. Some of the Pharisees heard these words and asked, "Are we blind also?" (v. 40). The Lord declared that the Pharisees who were so sure of their perception and discernment were indeed spiritually blind, and stood condemned in sin as well (v. 41).

9:22. For the synagogue see John 6:59 note.

9:35. For the title *Son of God* see John 1:34 note; for *believe* see John 1:7 note.

9:38. The formerly blind man worshipped the Lord Jesus. Thomas called Him "My Lord and my God" (20:28). The throne of God and of the Lamb will be in the heavenly city (Rev. 22:1). For the worship of the Lord Jesus Christ see Matt. 2:2, 11; 8:2; 9:18; 14:33; 15:25; Heb. 1:6. See also *ISBE*, "Worship," IV, pp. 1117–33; *ZPEB*, "Worship," V, pp. 969–990.

9:41. For spiritual blindness see *ISBE*, "Blindness," I, pp. 525–26.

Practical Applications from John 9

1. Afflictions do not come because of sin; they come as opportunities for God to work (John 9:3).
2. Obedience to God's word brings blessing (v. 7).
3. The fear of man twists the thinking of people (vv. 20–22).
4. The Lord Jesus received the worship of men (vv. 38–39).
5. Spiritual blindness is sin (v. 41).

Prayer

Dear Lord, give us spiritual perception. Help us to see Your hand in the events and circumstances of our day. Give us the boldness to confess You before men. Deliver us from a guilty silence. For Jesus' sake. Amen.

JOHN 10

Jesus, the Good Shepherd

Persons

Jesus
the Jews

Persons mentioned

a thief and robber
the shepherd
the porter
a stranger
the Good Shepherd
a hireling
a demon
the blind
the Father
the Christ
My sheep
John [the Baptist]

Places mentioned

the sheepfold
Jerusalem
Solomon's portico
a place beyond Jordan where John baptized

Doctrines taught

omniscience of the Shepherd
Jesus the Door of the sheep
Jesus the Door of salvation
Jesus the Good Shepherd
Jesus gives abundant life to His people
Jesus knows His sheep
Jesus can lay down His life and take it again
the unity of God's people: one fold
My sheep hear My voice
They shall never perish
"I and the Father, we are one thing" (10:30)
"The scripture cannot be broken" (10:35)
Jesus claimed, "I am the Son of God" (10:36)

John 10 Exposition

I. Jesus, the Good Shepherd. vv. 1–21.

The Lord Jesus entered by the door into the sheepfold. All others have been false shepherds and robbers. The sheep hear His voice. He calls each sheep by name and leads them out. It is still a striking thing to see a shepherd do this today. He goes before them, and the sheep follow him. He does not even look back to see if they are following; he knows they are coming. They will not follow a stranger (v. 5). The Lord goes on to declare, "Verily, verily, I say unto you, I am the door of the sheep" (v. 7). Modern readers sometimes miss the meaning of this statement. Ancient shepherds regularly built a fold for their sheep by piling up rocks in a circle high enough that a wolf could not jump over it. They left a doorway open through which the shepherd could lead his sheep in. When they were all accounted for, the shepherd would spread out his bedroll in the doorway and spend the night there. He was the door. Any wolf that came would have to climb over him to get to the sheep. It was a beautiful picture of the protective care of Christ for His people. Nothing can get past the Lord Jesus except by His permission. The believer can rest assured that the Lord is in full control and will protect him from all harm. The Lord promises, "I am the door: by me if any man enter in he shall be saved, and shall go in and out, and find pasture" (v. 9). He intends blessing for His people. The thief comes only to steal, kill, and destroy (v. 10). Jesus adds, "I am come that they might have life, and that they might have it more abundantly" (v. 10*b*). His purpose is always to bless His sheep. He claims, "I am the good shepherd: the good shepherd giveth his life for the sheep" (v. 11). The hireling will flee for his own safety (v. 12). He does not really care for the sheep (v. 13). In contrast the Lord

---

10:3. The "porter" was an under-shepherd who looked after the sheep when the shepherd had to be absent.

10:8. "All that came before" is a reference to false messiahs and would-be rulers who tried to deceive the people into following them.

10:11. The Lord Jesus is not only the Good Shepherd, but He is also "that great Shepherd of the sheep" (Heb. 13:20) and "the chief Shepherd" (I Pet. 5:4). All this refers back to David's words, "The Lord [Jehovah] is my shepherd" (Ps. 23:1), and to Isaiah's prophecy that the Lord Jehovah "shall feed his flock like a shepherd: he shall gather the lambs with his arm, and carry them in his bosom, and shall gently lead those that are with young" (Isa. 40:11). Asaph prayed, "Give ear, O Shepherd of Israel, thou that leadest Joseph like a flock . . . stir up thy strength, and come and save us" (Ps. 80:1–2). See *ZPEB*, "Shepherd," V, pp. 397–99; *ISBE*, "Sheep; Shepherd," IV, pp. 463–65; Butler, Trent, ed., *Holman Bible*

Jesus knows His sheep and is known by them (v. 14). God the Father knows the Son with infinite perfection, and the Son knows the heavenly Father with equal perfection (v. 15). He lays down His life for the sheep, Gentile sheep as well as Jewish sheep, and there shall be one fold, and one shepherd (v. 16). The Father loves the Son because of His self-sacrifice (v. 17). No man could take His life, but He lays it down willingly (v. 18). The Jews argue among themselves over the meaning of these statements (v. 19). Some think that He is demon-possessed or mad (v. 20). Others note that His words do not sound like those of a demon-possessed person, and how can a demon open the eyes of the blind (v. 21)?

II. Jesus at the Feast of Dedication. vv. 22–42.

The Feast of Dedication was a winter festival known as "the Feast of Lights," so called because of the lights the people kindled during the celebration. The Lord Jesus was walking in the eastern colonnade of the temple (v. 23), and the Jews came and encircled Him and were challenging Him: "If you are the Christ, say it to us boldly" (v. 24). Jesus answered them, "I said it to you, and you are not believing; the works which I am doing in my Father's name, these things are testifying concerning me" (v. 25). He went on to charge them, "But you are not believing, because you are not of my sheep" (v. 26). Now the Lord uses a series of present-tense verbs: "My sheep are hearing my voice, and I am knowing them, and they are following me, and I am giving them eternal life, and they shall never perish into the age, and no one shall snatch them out of my hand" (vv. 27–28). The concluding future tense is eternal security. The Lord explained, "My Father who has

---

Dictionary, "Shepherd," p. 1263; Harrison, R. K., ed., *The New Unger's Bible Dictionary*, "Shepherd," pp. 1179–80; Owen, G. Frederick, *The Shepherd Psalm of Palestine*, beautiful photographs.

10:15. Note the absolute omniscience that Jesus claimed.

10:27. The great characteristic of sheep is that they follow the shepherd. Goats tend to stray off.

10:30. The deity of Christ is emphasized over and over in John. There are 7 claims. He is the Word Who was God (1:1), the unique Son of God (1:34), and the only begotten Son (3:16). The Father has committed all judgment unto the Son (5:22). Christ claimed to be the "I AM" (8:58; Exod. 3:14) and said, "I and my Father, we are one thing" (10:30) and "I am in the Father, and the Father in me" (14:11). See *ISBE*, "Deity," I, pp. 913–14; *ZPEB*, "Deity of Christ," II, pp. 88–89; *NDBT*, "God," pp. 511–21.

given them to me, is greater than all, and no man is able to snatch them out of the hand of my Father. I and the Father, we are one thing" (vv. 29–30). He is plainly teaching the equal deity of both the Father and the Son. The Jews understood exactly what He was claiming and took up stones to stone Him (v. 31). But the Lord Jesus answered, "I showed you many good works from the Father; on account of which of them are you stoning me?" (v. 32). The Jews answered Him, "We are not stoning you for a good work, but for blasphemy, because you, being a man, are making yourself God" (v. 33). Jesus answered them, "Has it not been written in your law, 'I said, ye are gods' [Ps. 82:6]? If he called them gods, to whom the word of God came, and the Scripture cannot be broken, are you saying of him whom the Father sanctified and sent into the world, You are blaspheming, because I said, I am the Son of God?" (vv. 34–36). The eternal salvation of men depends on their faith in the Lord Jesus Christ (1:12) and in His works (vv. 37–38). He declared clearly Who He was, and His works proved His claim. The Lord Jesus escaped out of their hand and went away beyond Jordan (v. 40). Many believed on Him there (v. 42).

Practical Applications from John 10

1. Sheep know the voice of their shepherd; God's sheep need to know His voice (vv. 4–5).
2. The Lord Jesus is the Door, the only path to God and heaven (vv. 7–9).
3. The Lord intends His people to have abundant life (v. 10).

10:34. The human rulers in Israel were called "gods" because of their exalted human position, but they would die like any other human beings (Ps. 82:6). Jesus could be called God in a much more realistic sense. See the *Apologetics Study Bible*, p. 1592.

10:35. "The Scripture cannot be broken" is an absolute assumption by the Lord Jesus of the verbal inspiration of the Bible. It is not possible for the Scripture to err in any truth. The God Who inspired the Book is omniscient. He would not deceive or mislead anyone. For discussion see Custer, *Does Inspiration Demand Inerrancy?*; Edward Young, *Thy Word Is Truth*; B. B. Warfield, *The Inspiration and Authority of the Bible*; T. E. Engelder, *Scripture Cannot Be Broken*; Robert Lightner, *The Savior and the Scripture*. See also *ZPEB*, "Inspiration," III, pp. 286–93; *ISBE*, "Inspiration," II, pp. 839–49. The fact that unbelievers deny the doctrine is hardly surprising. The Book condemns them (Rom. 2:8–9).

10:42. Believing in the Lord Jesus Christ is one of the main themes of John's Gospel: John 1:7, 12; 2:11; 3:15–18; 5:24; 6:35; 7:38–39; 8:24; 9:35; 11:25–27; 12:44–47; 13:19; 14:1, 10–12; 16:27–31; 17:20–21; 20:29–31. See *ISBE*, "Faith," II, pp. 270–73; *ZPEB*, "Faith, Faithfulness," II, pp. 479–91.

4. The Good Shepherd knows His sheep, and they know Him (v. 14).
5. At the end the people of God will be one flock (v. 16).
6. Note present tense verbs: "My sheep keep hearing my voice, and I keep knowing them, and they keep following me, and I keep giving them eternal life" (John 10:27–28*a*).
7. "I and my Father, we are one thing" (v. 30); the unity of the divine nature.
8. "And the Scripture cannot be broken" (v. 35) denotes the divine inspiration and inerrancy of the Bible. See Custer, *Does Inspiration Demand Inerrancy?*

Prayer

Dear Lord, help Your people to humbly follow Your leading. Protect us from the wolves. Thank You that the Scripture cannot be broken. Give us grace to humbly follow You alone. For Jesus' sake. Amen.

JOHN 11

The Raising of Lazarus

Persons

Lazarus
Mary
Martha
the Lord Jesus
Thomas Didymus
the Pharisees
the chief priests
Caiaphas

Persons mentioned

the disciples
a man walking
the Jews
a council
the Romans
the people

Places mentioned

Bethany
Judea
Jerusalem
the house
the grave
the wilderness
the city Ephraim

Doctrines taught

the love of Christ
the Son of God
the glory of God
Jesus wept (shared their sorrow)
Jesus has power to raise the dead

John 11 Exposition

I. The Raising of Lazarus. vv. 1–46.

Lazarus, brother of Mary and Martha, was very sick, and the sisters sent to Jesus to let Him know (vv. 1–3). When Jesus heard, He said, "This sickness is not unto death, but for the glory of God" (v. 4). Jesus loved the three members of that family (v. 5). Yet it was only after two days that He went to Bethany (vv. 6–7). The disciples worried because the Jews had sought to stone Jesus (v. 8). But the Lord replied that those who walk in the light do not stumble (v. 9). He went on to say, "Our friend Lazarus sleepeth; but I go, that I may awake him out of sleep" (v. 11). The disciples thought that Jesus meant literal sleep and thought that Lazarus would get well (v. 12). But Jesus said plainly, "Lazarus is dead" (v. 14). He was glad that He was not there because He wanted the disciples to learn something (v. 15). Thomas, pessimistically thinking of the danger, said, "Let us also go, that we may die with him" (v. 16). When Jesus came, He found that Lazarus had been in the grave for four days already (v. 17). Many Jews came to comfort Martha and Mary (v. 19). Martha met the Lord and expressed faith that the Lord could have prevented her brother's death (vv. 20–21). She still had faith in Jesus (v. 22). The Lord promised, "Thy brother shall rise again" (v. 23). She expressed her faith in the resurrection at the last day (v. 24). The Lord declared, "I am the resurrection, and the life: he that believeth in me, though he were dead, yet shall he live: and whosoever liveth and believeth in me shall never die. Believest thou this?" (vv. 25–26). Martha confessed, "Yea, Lord: I believe that thou art the Christ, the Son of God, which should come into the world" (v. 27). She still did not see how that affected

---

11:1. Bethany is a village 2 miles southeast of Jerusalem (v. 18). See *ZPEB*, "Bethany," I, pp. 527–29; *ISBE*, "Bethany," I, pp. 463–64; John McRay, *Archaeology and the New Testament*, pp. 195–98.

For Lazarus see *ISBE*, "Lazarus," III, pp. 94–95; *ZPEB*, "Lazarus of Bethany," III, pp. 897–99; Harrison, R. K., ed., *Unger's Bible Dictionary*, "Lazarus," #2, p. 765. For Mary see *ZPEB*, "Mary of Bethany," IV, p. 104; *ISBE*, "Mary," #2, IV, p. 268. For Martha see *ZPEB*, "Martha," IV, pp. 102–3; *ISBE*, "Martha," III, pp. 266–67.

11:16. Thomas was despondent. For "die with him" see *ZPEB*, "Martyr," IV, p. 103; *ISBE*, "Martyr," III, p. 267. A martyr was a person so serious in his testimony for Christ that he would die for Him.

11:24. Martha had very orthodox faith in the resurrection but did not see how that applied to her present grief. The Lord Jesus is not only Lord over the future, but Lord over all present circumstances as well. People sin at their own risk.

her present grief. Martha notified Mary privately, "The Master is come, and calls for thee" (v. 28). Mary went out quickly to meet the Lord (vv. 29–30). She fell at His feet, saying, "Lord, if thou hadst been here, my brother had not died" (v. 32). The Lord Jesus saw the tears of the mourners and wept with them (vv. 33–35). The Jews exclaimed, "Behold how he loved him" (v. 36). The Lord Jesus commanded them to roll away the stone from the grave (v. 39). Martha exclaimed that Lazarus had been dead four days and by now the stench of death was overpowering. The Lord reminded her that He had said she would see the glory of God (v. 40). The Lord prayed to His Father and then cried with a loud voice, "Lazarus, come forth" (v. 43). Lazarus was propelled forth out of the tomb, still wrapped [like a mummy] with the grave clothes. He did not get up and walk out. The Lord then commanded, "Loose him, and let him go" (v. 44*b*). That entailed unwinding yards and yards of grave clothes. As a result of this miracle, many of the Jews believed on Him (v. 45). But some of the Jews went to the Pharisees and reported what Jesus had done (v. 46). That, however, did not move them to faith.

II. The Plotting to Kill Jesus. vv. 47–57.

The chief priests and the Pharisees gathered a council to kill Jesus (vv. 47ff.). Caiaphas argued that one man should die for the people (v. 50). Thus, unknowingly, he prophesied as high priest that Jesus should die for that nation (v. 51), just as Isaiah 53:8 had prophesied. But the Lord was to be a light to the Gentiles as well (Isa. 49:6). From that day there was a serious plot by the authorities to kill the Lord (v. 53). "Jesus therefore walked

---

11:35. "Jesus wept." This is the only time in John that Jesus is said to have wept. The Lord Jesus fully shared the sorrows and trials of His people. Here He wept over the death of Lazarus. However, Jesus is Lord over death as well as over life. See *ISBE*, "Weep; Weeping," IV, p. 1046; Ryken, Wilhoit, and Longman, *Dictionary of Biblical Imagery*, "Weeping," pp. 939–40.

11:43–44. The raising of Lazarus is not presented as reviving from fainting. He had been dead and in the grave for four days. The smell of corruption was evident. The Lord Jesus restored Lazarus back to life and health by His command. It was a supreme example of His divine power and authority.

11:48. The Pharisees feared that the Romans would hear of the miracles and come to put down the religious excitement.

11:50–51. Caiaphas is an example of a wicked man used to utter a prophecy that he did not understand. It was rare for a priest to prophesy anything. See *ZPEB*, "Caiaphas," I, pp. 683–85; *ISBE*, "Caiaphas," I, pp. 570–71.

no more openly among the Jews" (v. 54). Instead He withdrew near the wilderness. At the following Passover, crowds of the Jews gathered and sought for Jesus (v. 56). The chief priests and Pharisees had given a standing order that He be arrested (v. 57). But all their cautious preparation could not prevent the Lord from accomplishing the atoning sacrifice for His people.

Practical Applications from John 11

1. Divine love permits trials in the believer's life (11:6).
2. Some things happen to deliberately provoke the believer into faith (v. 15).
3. Faith in the eschatological future is not the same as faith for today (vv. 24–26).
4. The Lord Jesus fully shares the sorrows and trials of His people (v. 35).
5. Martha did not understand that what the Lord commanded always had a good purpose (v. 39).
6. The Lord did the impossible, but He would not do the work that others should do (v. 44).
7. The Jewish leaders feared loss of their place, but not the thought of murder (vv. 48–53).

Prayer

Dear Lord, help Your people to trust in You, even in times of trial and suffering. Enable us to see Your compassionate care in the midst of crisis. For Jesus' sake. Amen.

JOHN 12

Supper at Bethany; Triumphal Entry

Persons

- the Lord Jesus
- Martha
- Lazarus
- Mary
- Judas Iscariot
- the chief priests
- many people
- the King of Israel
- the Pharisees
- certain Greeks
- the prince of this world
- Philip
- Andrew
- God the Father
- Isaiah

Persons mentioned

- Simon (Judas' father)
- chief rulers
- an angel
- the children of light

Places mentioned

- Bethany
- Jerusalem
- Sion
- Bethsaida of Galilee
- Heaven

Doctrines taught

- being raised from the dead
- believing on Jesus
- the value of service
- the opportunity of praise
- the value of self-sacrifice
- spiritual blindness
- the fear of men
- the Word that judges
- life everlasting

John 12 Exposition

I. Mary, Martha, and Lazarus at Bethany. vv. 1–11.

Six days before the Passover Jesus came to Bethany to see Lazarus, Mary, and Martha. Martha was serving (Imperf. tense; continued action); Lazarus sat at the table with the Lord Jesus; and Mary came with a pound of ointment of spikenard, very costly (vv. 1–2). She anointed the feet of Jesus with the spikenard and wiped them with her hair (v. 3). Judas Iscariot asked why the ointment was not sold and the money given to the poor (v. 5). He did not care for the poor, but desired control over the money (v. 6). The Lord Jesus defended her action (vv. 7f.). People came just to see Lazarus (v. 9). The chief priests were so concerned that they considered putting Lazarus to death (vv. 10–11).

II. The Triumphal Entry. vv. 12–19.

On the next day a crowd of people took palm branches and went to meet Jesus, crying, "Hosanna: blessed is the King of Israel that cometh in the name of Lord" (v. 13; Ps. 118:25–26). The Lord Jesus rode upon an ass's colt (v. 14; see also Zech. 9:9). The disciples did not understand all these things at the time, but later they perceived the fulfillment of the Old Testament prophecies (v. 16). There were witnesses who testified that the Lord had raised Lazarus from the grave (v. 17). The news of the miracle drew crowds to see Him (v. 18). The Pharisees admit defeat: "The world is gone after him" (v. 19).

III. The Glorification of the Son of Man. vv. 20–50.

Certain Greeks desired to see Jesus, but that would come after the day of Pentecost (vv. 20–22; Acts 2). The Lord Jesus declared that the hour is

---

12:1. For Bethany see John 11:1 note.

12:3. Why did Mary wipe Jesus' feet with her hair? The spikenard was a powerful perfume. Women have traditionally put perfume on their hair. It is mentioned in the Song of Solomon (1:12; 4:13, 14). See *ZPEB*, "Spikenard," V, p. 502; *ISBE*, "Nard," III, pp. 490–91.

12:4. For Judas Iscariot see John 6:71 note.

12:6. The "bag" referred to a shepherd's bag, which might hold money, food, or whatever (see I Sam. 17:40, 49).

12:13. What does "Hosanna" mean? It means "Save, Lord" (see Ps. 118:25).

12:14–15. For ass see *ZPEB*, "Ass," I, pp. 366–68; *ISBE*, "Ass," I, p. 330.

come that the Son of man should be glorified (v. 23). That will be for the benefit of all nations. But the grain of wheat must fall into the ground and die in order to bring forth much fruit (v. 24). The Lord gives a paradox: he who loves his life shall lose it; he who hates his life in this world shall guard it unto life eternal (v. 25). "If anyone would serve me, let him follow me; and where I am there shall my servant be. If anyone serves me, him shall my Father honor" (v. 26). God will not forget a single act of service. The Lord considers whether He should ask for deliverance from the hour of suffering, but His purpose was to come for this very hour (v. 27). He prays, "Father, glorify thy name." And a voice came from heaven, "I have both glorified it, and will glorify it again" (v. 28). The people thought it thundered (v. 29). Jesus said, "This voice came . . . for your sakes" (v. 30). He went on to say, "Now is the judgment of this world." He was referring to the judgment for sin that would result in drawing all people toward Himself (vv. 31–32). He refers to the death on the cross (v. 33). Some people objected that Messiah should abide forever (v. 34). The day will come in which He shall judge the world in preparation for His reign (Matt. 25:31–46). The Lord said to them, "Walk while ye have the light, lest darkness come upon you" (v. 35*b*). Jesus then departed and hid Himself from them (v. 36). Although He did many signs, they did not believe in Him (v. 37); Isaiah the prophet had revealed this centuries before (v. 38; Isa. 53:1ff.). The prophecy of Isaiah was fulfilled, "He hath blinded their eyes, and hardened their heart; that they should not see with their eyes, nor understand with their heart, and be converted, and I should heal them" (v. 40; Isa. 6:10). Isaiah prophesied this "when he saw his glory, and spake of him" (v. 41, Isa. 6:1). Many among the chief rulers "believed on him; but because of the Pharisees they did not confess him, lest they should be put out of the synagogue: for they loved the praise of men more than the praise of God" (vv. 42*b*–43).

12:31. "The prince of this world" is a reference to Satan. See also John 14:30; Rev. 12:7–9.

12:32–33. This was a prophecy of His death on the cross. See *ISBE*, "Cross," I, pp. 825–30; *ZPEB*, "Cross," I, pp. 1037–39; *EDBT*, "Cross," pp. 136–37; Biedermann, Hans, *Dictionary of Symbolism*, "Cross," pp. 81–84.

12:43. For praise see *ZPEB*, "Praise," IV, p. 834; *ISBE*, "Praise," III, pp. 929–31.

The Lord cried out, "He that believeth on me, believeth not on me, but on him that sent me" (v. 44). The person who recognized the divine love and grace in Christ was perceiving the true nature of God the Father (v. 45). Faith in the Son honors the Father. Jesus cried, "I am come a light into the world, that whosoever believeth on me should not abide in darkness" (v. 46). But the Lord left a warning, "If any man hear my words, and guard them not, I judge him not: for I came not to judge the world, but to save the world" (v. 47). Then He severely warned, "He that rejecteth me, and receiveth not my words, hath one that judgeth him: the word that I have spoken, the same shall judge him in the last day" (v. 48). The Lord Jesus is not voicing a private, or merely human opinion, but the considered judgment of His heavenly Father (vv. 49–50).

Practical Applications from John 12

1. Judas suggested doing a good thing with the ointment, but not using it for the Lord Jesus (vv. 4–5).
2. The chief priests thought of murdering Lazarus just to discredit Jesus (vv. 10–11).
3. In the face of impending death the Lord Jesus does not pray to be delivered, but to glorify His heavenly Father (vv. 27–28).
4. The Lord Jesus knew that His death on the cross would draw men to God (v. 32).
5. Jesus urged, "While ye have the light, believe in the light." All men should seize the opportunity of being saved, lest they perish in unbelief (v. 36).
6. The fear of men's opinions can cause some to forfeit eternal salvation (vv. 42–43).

Prayer

Dear Lord, give us the courage to stand for You in the midst of a wicked world. Enable us to be a good testimony for You. For Jesus' sake. Amen.

12:44–45. There is an infinite, divine unity between the Persons of the Trinity. See Matt. 28:19 note; II Cor. 13:14 note.

12:46. For Jesus as a light see John 1:4 note.

JOHN 13

The Foot Washing

Persons

- Jesus
- Judas Iscariot
- the Devil, Satan
- Simon Peter
- the disciple Jesus loved (John)

Persons mentioned

- God the Father
- Simon (Judas' father)
- the poor
- the Jews

Places mentioned

- the Upper Room

Doctrines taught

- the love of God
- spiritual cleansing
- One of the apostles would betray Christ
- Jesus was glorified in the sacrifice of Himself
- Believers should love one another
- Love is the mark of Christ's disciples
- Peter was going to deny Christ three times

John 13 Exposition

I. The Foot Washing. vv. 1–20.

The Lord Jesus loved His disciples to the end (v. 1). The Devil had put into the heart of Judas the betrayal (v. 2). In full knowledge of that and of the Father's love, Jesus rose from the table, took a towel, poured water into a basin, and began to wash the disciples' feet (vv. 3–4). This is a staggering lesson in humility. The Lord of all stoops to wash the feet of His slaves. When He came to Simon Peter, Peter objected, "Thou shalt never wash my feet" (v. 8). But the Lord answered him, "If I wash thee not, thou hast no part with me." Peter then begged Him to wash his hands and head also (v. 9). But Jesus replied, He that is bathed (*louo*) has no need except to wash his feet. This is the imagery of one walking home from the bath-house. The Lord knew who the betrayer was (v. 11). The Lord said, "You are calling me 'the Teacher,' and 'the Lord,' and you are saying well, for I am" (v. 13). He goes on to say, "If I, the Lord and the Teacher, washed your feet, you ought to be washing the feet of one another" (v. 14). He has given believers an example of kindness for all time. He then said, "Amen, amen, I am saying to you that the slave is not greater than his lord, nor an apostle greater than the one who sent him. If you know these things, blessed are you if you keep on doing them" (vv. 16–17). He then said, "I am not

---

13:1. The Feast of the Passover was one of the most important festivals of the Jewish year. It celebrated the deliverance from the bondage of Egypt. See *ZPEB*, "Passover," IV, pp. 605–11; *ISBE*, "Passover," III, pp. 675–79; *EDBT*, "Feasts and Festivals of Israel," p. 249f.

13:2. Judas was a betrayer: although a disciple, Judas turned the Lord Jesus Christ over to His enemies. He did it secretly by night, with a kiss, for money, and in the knowledge of the Lord's innocence. See *ISBE*, "Betray; Betrayer," I, p. 480; Harrison, E. F., ed., *Baker's Dictionary of Theology*," Betrayal," pp. 93–94.

13:10. "He that is bathed (*louo*) needs not save to wash (*nipto*) his feet." *Nipto* means to wash the extremities. See *ISBE*, "Foot Washing," II, p. 333; *ZPEB*, "Foot Washing," II, p. 588. "It was not to observe a custom, for the disciples were mystified by it" (*ZPEB*, II, p. 588). The Lord was demonstrating His infinite love for His people. And so to this day the Lord cleanses His undeserving people. Christ gave Himself for the church "that he might sanctify and cleanse it with the washing of water by the word" (Eph. 5:26).

13:14. Jesus was much more than Lord and Master; He was also God the Son, our Redeemer and Savior. His example of humble service is astounding. Far too many believers think that humble service is beneath them.

13:16. The *slave* is not greater than his lord. He is not even a hired worker. Believers should not have too high an opinion of themselves.

speaking concerning you all, but that the scripture might be fulfilled: 'The one eating bread with me lifted up his heel against me'" (v. 18). He goes on to add, "Now I am saying these things to you before it happens, in order that whenever it comes to pass, you may believe that I am" (v. 19). The Lord is deliberately using the title of the Old Testament Jehovah God, "I Am" (Exod. 3:14). The Lord then says, "He that receives whomever I send, receives me; and he that receives me receives him who sent me" (v. 20). This is a great comfort to all soul winners.

II. The Lord's Teaching in the Upper Room. vv. 21–38.

The Lord Jesus was troubled (agitated) in spirit and declared plainly, "Verily, verily, I say unto you, that one of you shall betray me" (v. 21). The prophecy was in Psalm. 41:9, "Yea, mine own familiar friend, in whom I trusted, which did eat of my bread, hath lifted up his heel against me." The disciples looked at one another (v. 22). John was leaning on Jesus' breast and asked Him, "Lord, who is it?" (vv. 23–25). The Lord answered, "He it is, to whom I shall give a sop, when I have dipped it" (v. 26). The Lord gave it to Judas Iscariot, and then said to him, "That thou doest, do quickly" (v. 27). Judas was obviously sitting near the Lord, in a place of honor, but his heart was far away. The disciples had no idea what had happened (v. 28). As soon as Judas had left, the Lord declared, "Now is the Son of man glorified, and God is glorified in him" (v. 31). The atoning sacrifice for the sins of the world was sure to be made. In contrast to the hateful acts of Judas, the Lord declares, "A new commandment I give unto you, That ye love one another; as I have loved you, that ye also love one another" (v. 34). Christlike love will be the identifying mark of believers as disciples

---

13:26f. What was a "sop"? It was a piece of bread that had been dipped in the juices and gravy of the roast lamb. It was considered a great delicacy.

13:27. Satan is named only here in John. Demon possession is bad enough, but this was Satanic possession. Satan is that fallen angel who resists God's plan and seeks to destroy mankind. His ultimate destiny is to be cast into the lake of fire and brimstone (Rev. 20:10). See *ZPEB*, "Satan," V, pp. 282–86; *ISBE*, "Satan," IV, pp. 340–44; *EDBT*, "Satan," pp. 714–15; Louis Sperry Chafer, *Satan*; van der Toorn, Becking, and Vander Horst, *Dictionary of Deities and Demons in the Bible*, "Satan," pp. 726–32.

13:30. The night in Judas' soul was much darker than the night outside. Satan was in control (v. 27). See *ISBE*, "Betray; Betrayer," I, pp. 480–81; "Judas Iscariot," II, pp. 1151–53; *ZPEB*, "Judas Iscariot," III, p. 732; Harrison, E. F., ed., *Baker's Dictionary of Theology*, "Betrayal," pp. 93–94.

of Christ (v. 35; I Cor. 13). Peter asked the Lord where He was going, but Jesus told him that he could not follow now, but afterwards he would follow (vv. 36–37). The Lord warned Peter that he would deny Christ three times (v. 38). Peter did not believe it then, but it did happen (18:25–27). Peter had good intentions, but no power to achieve them.

Practical Applications from John 13

1. Judas was listening to the Devil's temptations (v. 2).
2. The Lord knew that every disciple needed cleansing in order to serve God (vv. 5ff.).
3. Divine cleansing is absolutely necessary for believers to be saved (v. 8).
4. Believers should regard Jesus as "Master and Lord" (v. 13).
5. The person who receives the messenger of the Lord receives the Lord Himself (v. 20).
6. The Lord Jesus commanded all believers to keep on loving one another (Pres. tense). We must never stop.

Prayer

Dear Lord, put Your love in our hearts so that it may overflow to others. Protect us from selfishness and unconcern. For Jesus' sake. Amen.

JOHN 14

The Upper Room Discourse

Persons

Jesus Christ
God the Father
Thomas
Philip
the Spirit (Comforter)
Judas (not Iscariot)

Persons mentioned

God
the person who loves Christ
the person who does not love Christ
the prince of this world (the Devil)

Places mentioned

My Father's house
many mansions
the world
the Upper Room (in "let us go hence")

Doctrines taught

faith in God
dwelling places in heaven
Christ will come again
Christ is the way, the truth, and the life
No man comes to the Father but by Jesus
The Spirit shall be in believers
The Father and Christ will come to the person who loves Christ
Christ will send the Comforter (another Comforter) to teach you all things
Christ leaves peace with believers

John 14 Exposition

I. The Promise of a Prepared Place. vv. 1–14.

The Lord urges His disciples, "Let not your heart be troubled; you believe in God; keep believing also in me" (14:1). Jesus taught that in His Father's house are many dwelling places; He goes to prepare a place for believers (v. 2). He also promises, "I will come again, and receive you unto myself; that where I am, there ye may be also" (v. 3). Being received into the courts of heaven is one of the most astonishing promises in the Bible. The Lord goes on to declare, "Whither I go ye know, and the way ye know" (v. 4). Thomas objects on both counts: he does not know where the Lord is going nor the way there (v. 5). The Lord gives him one of the great "I am" sayings: "I am the way, the truth, and the life: no man cometh unto the Father, but by me" (v. 6). The Lord Jesus Christ is the Way to God; there are no alternative ways. He is the Truth; all other religions are human fictions. He is the Life; all other religions lead to eternal death in the lake of fire (Rev. 20:11–15). The Lord goes on to say, "If you had known me, you would have known my Father also. And from now on you are knowing Him and have seen Him" (v. 7). He is referring to His own personal manifestation of the character of His Father. Philip boldly asks, "Lord, show us the Father" (v. 8). The Lord responds patiently, "Have I been with you so long a time, and you have not known me, Philip? The one who has seen me has seen the Father" (v. 9). The infinite love and patience that they had seen in

---

14:1. The verb *to trouble* means "to disturb, unsettle, terrify." See John 5:7; Acts 17:8; I Pet. 3:14. "The heart is the seat of spiritual life" (A. T. Robertson, *Word Pictures*, V, p. 248). See also Ps. 19:14; 27:8; 57:7; 119:10, 36.

14:2. "Many dwelling places." The Lord is speaking of heavenly dwelling places. Jesus taught that if a man loves Him, He and His Father will come and make their *dwelling place* with him (14:23).

14:2–3. The only time that the verb *to prepare* occurs in John's Gospel is in these two verses. The Lord's preparation is going to be spectacular (Rev. 21–22).

14:3. "I will come again." This is a specific promise of His coming for His people (I Thess. 4:13–18).

14:6. "Without the Way, there is no going; without the Truth, there is no knowing; without the Life, there is no living" (Thomas A. Kempis, *The Imitation of Christ*, p. 253).

14:7. The Lord addressed His Father as "Holy Father" and "righteous Father" (17:11, 25). For works on God the Father see John 1:14 note.

14:8. For Philip the apostle see John 1:43 note.

the Lord Jesus is in the Father as well. The Lord said clearly, "The Father that dwells in me is doing his works" (v. 10*b*). He urged, "Keep believing me that I am in the Father and the Father is in me" (v. 11). He declared most solemnly, "Amen, Amen, I am saying to you, the one who is believing in me, the works that I am doing shall that one do, and greater works than these shall he do, because I am going to the Father" (v. 12). The Son will be interceding for His servants and empowering their service. "And whatever you shall ask in my name, I will do it, that the Father may be glorified in the Son. If you ask anything in my name, I will do it" (vv. 13–14). The Lord is assuring His servants that He will be the One Who is accomplishing their service for Him. Believers should never think that they are struggling along alone in serving the Lord.

II. The Promise of the Holy Spirit. vv. 15–26.

"If you love me, keep my commandments; and I shall ask the Father and He shall give you another Comforter, that He may be with you forever" (vv. 15–16). Love for Christ must be the motivating power for the believer's obedience. The Comforter is "the Spirit of truth, whom the world is not able to receive, because it does not see or know him; you are knowing him, because he is abiding with you, and shall be in you" (v. 17). It was not until the day of Pentecost that the Spirit came upon all believers (Acts 2). The Lord assures believers, "I will not leave you orphans: I am coming to you" (v. 18). He gives another solemn promise to believers: "Because I live, you shall live also" (v. 19*b*). That life includes a promise of the indwelling Presence of God: "In that day you shall know that I am in my Father, and you in me, and I in you" (v. 20). He goes on to say, "The one who has my commandments and keeps them, he is the one who loves me; but the one who

---

14:13. What does "in my name" mean? Westcott suggests that it means "as being one with me even as I am revealed to you" (*John*, p. 204). See also *ISBE*, "Name," III, pp. 480–83; *ZPEB*, "Name," IV, pp. 360–66.

14:16. The "Comforter" is the Holy Spirit, "one called alongside to help" (*Paraclete*). Note also v. 26. See *ZPEB*, "Holy Spirit," III, pp. 183–96; *ISBE*, "Holy Spirit," II, pp. 730–46; *EDBT*, "Holy Spirit," pp. 344–48; *NDBT*, "Holy Spirit," pp. 551–58; Walvoord, John F., *The Holy Spirit*; Pache, René, *The Person and Work of the Holy Spirit*.

14:18. For *orphan, comfortless,* see *ISBE*, "Orphan," III, pp. 616–17; *ZPEB*, "Orphan," IV, pp. 546–48. The word means "desolate, bereft of parents" (Robertson, *Word Pictures*, vol. V, p. 253). The only other occurrence in Scripture is James 1:27.

loves me shall be loved by my Father, and I shall love him and manifest myself to him" (v. 21). The Lord knows the difference between a person who has a Bible that just sits on the shelf and a person who reads and obeys the Word out of love for the Lord Jesus. Judas, not Iscariot, asked how the Lord could manifest Himself to believers and not to the world (v. 22). Jesus answered and said to him, "If any one loves me, and shall keep my word, my Father also shall love him, and we shall come to him and we shall make our dwelling place with him" (v. 23). Paul phrased it, "I live; yet not I, but Christ liveth in me" (Gal. 2:20). This is a staggering privilege for any believer. The Lord also turns the truth around: "The one who is not loving me is not keeping my words, and the word which you hear is not mine but the Father's, who sent me" (v. 24). And so the disobedience is not merely against the Son, but against the Father as well. "But the Comforter, the Holy Spirit, whom the Father shall send in my name, that One shall teach you all things and shall remind you of all things which I said to you" (v. 26). The indwelling presence of the Holy Spirit instructs the believer and moves him ever closer to walk with God.

III. The Promise of Peace. vv. 27–31.

The Lord gives His peace to His people. In the midst of the wicked world they can have His peace. Because Jesus is Lord of all, circumstances should not trouble believers. No trials can reach them except the ones He intends for their good. Part of the disciples' coming ministry would be to preach the peace with God that comes through the Lord Jesus Christ (Rom. 5:1). Now He is ready to return to the Presence of His Father. The prince of this world (v. 30) is the Devil, who comes to try to destroy Christ but will only accomplish the redemptive sacrifice for the sins of the world. The command "Arise, let us go hence" shows that the rest of the discourse is spoken on the way across Jerusalem to Gethsemane.

14:21. The Father loves those who love His Son (16:27).

14:23. "Dwelling place" harks back to v. 2. The obedient, loving believer is one of the Father's many mansions!

14:27. *Peace* occurs 6 times in John (14:27; 16:33; 20:19, 21, 26). For more on "peace" see *ZPEB*, "Peace," IV, pp. 666–68; *ISBE*, "Peace," III, pp. 731–33; *EDBT*, "Peace," pp. 597–98; *NDBT*, "Peace," pp. 682–83.

This is the only time that this verb *to be afraid* (*deiliao*) occurs in the NT.

14:30. For Satan, the Devil, the "prince of this world," see John 13:27 note.

Practical Applications from John 14

1. The prepared dwelling place is in the immediate Presence of God (v. 2). It is our present task to learn how to live in the Presence of God while we are still in the present world. The Lord will come for His people when the "place" is prepared (v. 3).
2. The Lord declares, "I am the way, the truth, and the life: no man cometh unto the Father, but by me" (v. 6). Christ is the whole of salvation for the believer.
3. The Lord Jesus is the perfect revelation of God the Father (v. 9).
4. The Lord invites believers to pray to the Father in His name (v. 13).
5. He promises to send another Comforter, the Spirit of truth (vv. 16–17).
6. He stresses that our love for Him can be shown by keeping His commandments (v. 21).
7. He pronounces a benediction of peace on the believer (v. 27).

Prayer

Dear Lord, help us to think of You, and to walk with You, and talk with You along the pathway homeward. For Jesus' sake. Amen.

JOHN 15

Abiding in Christ

Persons

Jesus Christ
God the Father
the Spirit of truth

Persons mentioned

ye (disciples)
You (believers) are My friends (v. 14)
those who abide not in Me (apostates)

Places mentioned

the world
in Me

Doctrines taught

Christ is the True Vine
Genuine branches are pruned
Abide in Christ to bear fruit
Love one another
no cloak for sin
The Spirit of truth is the Comforter Who testifies of Christ

John 15 Exposition

I. Abiding in Christ. vv. 1–17.

On the way to the garden of Gethsemane the Lord continues His instruction. Christ is the true Vine; His Father is the Farmer; and believers are the branches (vv. 1–2). A branch that is broken off from a vine will die. The believer must realize that his relationship to God is of absolute importance. No believer can live a holy life without the power of God flowing through him. If he is going to have a fruitful testimony, God must do it through him. Believers are clean through the word of Christ (v. 3). Paul wrote that Christ cleansed the church by "the washing of water by the word" (Eph. 5:26*b*). Christ and the disciples may well have been walking past vineyards, or at least vines planted by the houses. The Lord commands every believer, "Abide in me, and I in you" (v. 4*a*). Christian service, soul winning, and daily testimony all depend on drawing strength from the Lord Jesus Christ. Just as the root of the vine keeps pouring strength into the branches, so the Lord must continue pouring His grace and strength into the believer if he is to have a testimony for Christ. The Lord declares clearly, "Without me ye can do nothing" (v. 5*b*). There is no service the believer can perform for Christ without abiding in Christ and drawing strength from Him. Abiding in Christ and letting His words abide in you is a powerful means of getting answered prayer (v. 7). The Lord desires much fruit from the believer (v. 8). The flow of divine love is clear: from the Father to the Son, to the believer, to other believers (v. 9). Obedience to God's commandments brings the

---

15:1–5. This is the central NT passage on the believer as a branch of the vine. In Israel people often have a grapevine growing in their front yard or by their backdoor. The idea of God's people being His vine is also found in Isa. 5:1–7; Ps. 80:8, 14–16. See *ZPEB*, "Vine, Vineyard," V, pp. 882–84; *ISBE*, "Vine," IV, pp. 986–87; Ryken, Wilhoit, and Longman, *Dictionary of Biblical Imagery*, "Vine, Vineyard," pp. 914–17.

15:2. The word *fruit* "expresses the productive quality of the life of a servant people" (*ISBE*, "Fruit," II, p. 365). See also *EDBT*, "Fruit," p. 274. The vine branches must be pruned so that they will bring forth abundant fruit. Believers would like to avoid the pruning, but it is necessary for fruitfulness, both in plants and people.

15:4–10. This is the major passage on the necessity of the believer abiding in Christ. A. T. Robertson writes, "The only way to continue 'clean' (pruned) and to bear fruit is to maintain vital spiritual connexion with Christ (the vine)" (*Word Pictures*, vol. V, p. 258). The word *abide* means to "maintain unbroken fellowship" (Harrison, E. F., ed., *Baker's Dictionary of Theology*, "Abide," p. 15). John also emphasizes *abiding* in I John 2:6–28; 3:6. See *ZPEB*, "Abide," I, p. 12; Murray, Andrew, *Abide in Christ*, 223 pp.

believer abiding love and joy (vv. 10–11). Christ commanded believers, "Love one another, as I have loved you" (v. 12). He goes on to comment, "Greater love hath no man than this, that a man lay down his life for his friends" (v. 13). The Lord expects obedience from His disciples (v. 14). The Lord assures believers that they are not slaves, but rather friends to whom He explains the will of His Father (v. 15). He also declares that they have not chosen Him; He has chosen them and ordained that they bring forth fruit that will remain (v. 16). That fruit surely includes winning souls to the Savior. And He commands that they continue loving one another (v. 17).

II. Dealing with the Hatred of the World. vv. 18–27.

Christ declared, "If the world hates you, you know that it has hated me before you" (v. 18). The wicked world hated Christ enough to kill Him. "If you were of the world, the world would love its own; but because you are not of the world, but I chose you out of the world, on account of this the world is hating you" (v. 19). The Lord warned the apostles that if "people have persecuted me, they will also persecute you" (v. 20). They will do this because they do not know God the Father (v. 21). The Lord had declared to the world the will of His Father. Now they are responsible: "They have no cloak for their sin" (v. 22). The person who hates Jesus Christ hates God the Father as well, for Jesus is the perfect manifestation of His Father (v. 23). The Lord Jesus solemnly warned that "now have they both seen and hated both me and my Father" (v. 24*b*). They did this according to the prophecy "They hated me without a cause" (v. 25; Ps. 69:4). Worldly people have all received many gracious gifts from God, yet they hate Him and refuse to obey Him.

The Lord then gave a prophecy: "But when the Comforter is come, whom I will send unto you from the Father, even the Spirit of truth, which

---

15:12, 17. The love of believers for other believers is not merely a good option, but a clear command by the Lord Jesus Christ Himself. If other believers are "difficult," we must remember that in the sight of God we are also.

15:18. The "World" is the evil cosmos, not just the planet. See *ZPEB*, "World," V, pp. 963–68; *ISBE*, "World," IV, pp. 1112–16; *EDBT*, "World," pp. 836–37; *NDBT*, "World," pp. 853–55.

15:19. Because Christ has chosen His people out of the world, the world hates them with peculiar virulence. Worldly people can overlook grievous faults in one another, but they relish pouncing on the slightest misstep by a believer.

proceedeth from the Father, he shall testify of me" (v. 26). Thus the Lord authenticated the New Testament writings that were yet to come. Peter assures us, "For the prophecy came not in old time by the will of man: but holy men of God spake as they were moved by the Holy Ghost" (II Pet. 1:21). So the Lord assures believers that the New Testament writings will be verbally inspired in the same way. The Holy Spirit is responsible for the content of the New Testament. He is the "Spirit of truth" (14:17). The man who calls Him a liar will have to face Him at the last Judgment. For the doctrine of the verbal inspiration of the Scriptures, see John 10:35 note.

Practical Applications from John 15

1. "Abide in me" is the Lord's command to every believer. We are to maintain a constant spiritual contact with the Lord, drawing from Him every spiritual grace and strength that we need (John 15:4).
2. Abiding in Christ empowers our prayers (v. 7).
3. Believers should glorify their heavenly Father by bearing much fruit (v. 8).
4. Believers should abide in the love of Christ (v. 9), and they will find that His joy abides in them (v. 11).
5. It is Christ's will that His joy might abide in believers and their joy might be full (v. 11).
6. Christ does not call believers slaves, but rather friends, chosen and loved (vv. 15–16).
7. When the Comforter, the Spirit of truth, comes, He shall testify of Christ (v. 26).

Prayer

Dear Lord, help us to constantly abide in You, and to let Your Spirit abide in us to do all Your will. For Jesus' sake. Amen.

15:26. "The Comforter" is one of the major titles of God the Holy Spirit. See also John 14:16, 26; 15:26; 16:7. See *ZPEB*, "Holy Spirit," III, pp. 183–96; *ISBE*, "Paraclete," III, pp. 659–60; *EDBT*, "Holy Spirit," pp. 344–48; Walvoord, John, *The Holy Spirit*, 275 pp.; Swete, Henry Barclay, *The Holy Spirit in the New Testament*, 417 pp.; Thomas, William B. Griffith, *The Holy Spirit of God*, 303 pp.

JOHN 16

The Ministry of the Spirit

Persons

Jesus Christ
the disciples
God the Father
the Comforter (the Spirit of Truth)
the prince of this world (the Devil)

Persons mentioned

rulers of synagogues
unbelievers
a woman in labor

Places mentioned

synagogues
the world

Doctrines taught

Persecution shall come
It is profitable for believers that Christ go away
The Comforter will convict the world of sin
Disciples will have sorrow, but also joy
The Spirit is our Guide
Praying in Jesus' name brings answers
In the world believers will have tribulation, but Jesus has conquered the world

John 16 Exposition

I. The Ministry of the Holy Spirit. vv. 1–15.

The Lord Jesus is giving the disciples this teaching so that they will understand the teaching about Himself and the Father and the reason for the discrimination that they must endure. Their enemies know nothing about God and His will (vv. 2–3). Jesus is also giving the disciples this teaching because He is about to leave them and return to His Heavenly Father (v. 5). The disciples were sorrowful to hear that He was going away (v. 6). But the Lord assures them that it is profitable for them that He go away, for He is going to send them the Comforter (the Holy Spirit, v. 7). The Comforter is going to convict the world of three things: sin, righteousness, and judgment (v. 8). He will convict the world of the sin of unbelief (v. 9); of righteousness because the righteous Lord will return to His Father (v. 10); and of judgment because the prince (ruler) of this world has been judged (v. 11). Obviously judgment awaits the wicked who follow Satan. He stands condemned, awaiting the lake of fire (Rev. 20:10). He continues opposing the work of God, but there is nothing he can do to avoid his final judgment. The Lord Jesus had much more to say, but He refers the disciples to the Spirit of truth. The Spirit will reveal to them all the teaching of the New Testament books (vv. 12–13). The Spirit will glorify the Lord Jesus and manifest Him

---

16:1–2. The Lord Jesus spoke these words in order to protect His people. Persecution is coming to believers. They will be put out of the synagogues and martyred. These things will happen because the proud persecutors do not know the Lord Jesus or God the Father.

16:4. When persecution comes, believers should remember that the Lord had warned them.

16:7. See John 14:16 note for the Comforter.

16:8. The ministry of the Holy Spirit is to convict the world of sin, of [their lack] of righteousness, and of [coming] judgment. The prince of this world has been judged (condemned, v. 11). But the ministry of the Holy Spirit is also to sanctify believers (vv. 12–15). He sets them apart for God. See *ISBE*, "Sanctification," IV, pp. 321–31; *ZPEB*, "Sanctification," V, pp. 264–67; *EDBT*, "Sanctification," pp. 708–13.

16:13. The Holy Spirit is going to guide believers into all truth. This began with His revelation of the 27 New Testament books. It surely continued with His illumination of godly expositors, teachers, and preachers who seek His guidance in the interpretation and proclamation of His holy Word. Unbelieving theologians and preachers who deny the doctrines of Scripture have no such illumination. They deny the Lord and the Scriptures because they do not know Him as Savior. To them He is merely the "man of Galilee." The Lord Jesus Himself warned, "Beware of false prophets, which come to you in sheep's clothing, but inwardly they are ravening wolves" (Matt. 7:15). It is the Holy Spirit Himself Who imparts the fruit of the Spirit: "love, joy, peace, longsuffering, gentleness, goodness, faith, meekness, temperance" (Gal. 5:22–23). See Walvoord, John F., *The Holy Spirit*;

to believers (v. 14). All that the Father has He has given to the Son, and so it is the Son Who shall manifest all things to believers (v. 15).

II. The Lord's Explanation. vv. 16–33.

The Lord said cryptically, "A little while, and ye shall not see me: and again, a little while, and ye shall see me, because I go to the Father" (v. 16). This statement puzzled the disciples (vv. 16–18). But the Lord explained that in a little while He would die and the disciples would weep and lament while the wicked world would rejoice (v. 20); but the disciples' sorrow would be turned into joy by His victory over death (vv. 21–22). He gives a great promise: "Whatsoever ye shall ask the Father in my name, he will give it you" (v. 23*b*). He urges them, "Keep on asking [pres.], and ye shall receive, that your joy may be full" (v. 24*b*). He promises them, "The time comes when I shall no more speak in proverbs, but I shall show you plainly of the Father" (v. 25). He had taught them much in parables, but now He is going to reveal further doctrinal truth in the Epistles that will follow. He assures them that "the Father himself loves you, because you have loved me, and have believed that I came out from God" (v. 27). He then gives them a summary of His ministry. "I came forth from the Father and have come into the world; again I leave the world, and go to the Father" (v. 28). The disciples respond that He is now very clear (v. 29), and assure the Lord that they believe "that thou camest forth from God" (v. 30). The Lord asks, "Are you now believing?" (v. 31). They did not understand how shattering the death of the Lord would be to their hopes and plans (v. 32). The Lord will face death alone, and He will accomplish the redemptive sacrifice for the sins of the world (v. 33). He assures them, "Be of good cheer; I have

---

Pache, René, *The Person and Work of the Holy Spirit*; Swete, Henry Barclay, *The Holy Spirit in the New Testament*, for further study.

16:21–24. Part of the fruit of the Spirit is joy (Gal. 5:22; I Pet. 1:8; I John 1:4). Paul mentions his joy in the midst of affliction (II Cor. 7:4–16). See *ISBE*, "Joy," II, pp. 1140–42; *ZPEB*, "Joy," III, pp. 714–15; *EDBT*, "Joy," pp. 430–31.

16:23. The assurance that prayer will be answered when it is offered in Jesus' name (in submission to His authority) is one of the greatest blessings that believers could have. See *ZPEB*, "Prayer," IV, pp. 835–44; *ISBE*, "Prayer," III, pp. 931–39; Murray, Andrew, *With Christ in the School of Prayer*; Bounds, E. M., *The Necessity of Prayer*; Henry, Matthew, *The Quest for Communion With God*; Hiebert, D. Edmond, *Working with God Through Prayer*; Murray, Andrew, *Abide in Christ*.

16:27. The infinite love of the Father for those who love His Son is one of the most precious revelations of the Lord Jesus.

conquered the world" (v. 33). His divine power will yet conquer the world. The world will not be left as a monument to Satan's power, but as a monument to the grace and love of an Almighty Savior.

Practical Applications from John 16

1. The Lord warned about future persecution (John 16:2–3).
2. It is profitable that the Lord has gone back to heaven because now He has sent the Comforter to empower our testimony (vv. 7–11).
3. He promises that the Spirit will guide believers into all truth (v. 13).
4. In this life we have sorrow, but in that life we will have joy in His presence forever (vv. 22ff.).
5. The Father loves believers because they love His Son (v. 27).
6. Believers may be of good cheer because Christ has conquered the world (v. 33).

Prayer

Dear Lord, give us grace to endure the trials of this life, and give the assurance of complete victory in Thee in the world to come. For Jesus' sake. Amen.

16:32–33. The Lord knew the devastating effect His death would have on the disciples, but He also knew that His resurrection would change everything for them. It is in Jesus alone that believers have peace and victory.

JOHN 17

The High-Priestly Prayer

Persons

Jesus Christ
God the Father (Holy Father, Righteous Father)

Persons mentioned

all flesh
the men Thou hast given Me
the son of perdition (Judas)

Places mentioned

Heaven
the world

Doctrines taught

the importance of prayer
intercessory prayer
eternal life: knowing God
glorifying God
the keeping power of God
sanctification through the truth of the Word
the unity of believers
the beatific vision of the glory of Christ

John 17 Exposition

I. Christ Prays the Father to Glorify the Son. vv. 1–5.

The Lord does not pray that His Father spare Him from suffering; He came to suffer and die for the sins of the world. He prays that the Father would glorify His Son. He notes that the Father has given Him authority over all flesh, that He should give eternal life to as many as the Father has given Him (v. 2). He is the only human being Who can impart eternal life. He defines eternal life as knowing "thee the only true God, and Jesus Christ, whom thou hast sent" (v. 3). A personal, eternal relationship with God is the true goal of mankind's existence. The Lord Jesus glorified His Father on the earth, and with the cross He will finish His work on earth (v. 4). Now He prays the Father to restore His eternal glory (v. 5). That prayer was answered in His Resurrection (Acts 1:8–11; Rev. 5:5–12).

II. He Prays for the People the Father Has Given Him. vv. 6–19.

The Lord manifested the name (character) of His Father to believers, and He emphasizes that they have kept God's Word (v. 6). They know that His gifts and powers are from God the Father (v. 7). They have received His words as words from the Father (v. 8). Unbelievers who deny that the Lord prayed this prayer are placing themselves outside the pale of salvation. All true believers belong to both the Father and the Son (vv. 9–10). The Lord intercedes for true believers, not the world (v. 9). Now the Lord is going to leave the world and return to the Father ("I am coming to thee," v. 11*a*).

17:1–26. A. T. Robertson answers the doubting critics by writing, "It is inconceivable that this real *Lord's Prayer* is the free composition of a disciple put into the mouth of Jesus. It is rather 'the tenacious memory of an old man recalling the greatest days of his life' (Bernard)" (*Word Pictures*, V, p. 274). For a heart-warming exposition of this chapter see Marcus Rainsford, *Our Lord Prays for His Own*, 476 pp.

17:3. Knowing the Trinitarian God is life eternal. Since He is infinite, it will be a never-ending joy of learning wisdom and trust in God. *ZPEB*, "Know, Knowledge," III, pp. 836–40; *ISBE*, "Know," III, pp. 48–50; *EDBT*, "Know, Knowledge," pp. 457–58; "Knowledge of God," pp. 458–59.

17:4. The change in tenses is striking: "I glorified [Aor.] thee upon the earth, having completed [Aor.] the work which thou hast given [Perf.] me that I should do it [Aor. Subjunc.]. The solemn trust which the Father gave to the Son will be thoroughly completed.

17:6. "They have kept [Perf. tense, with continuing results] thy word."

17:9. The Lord did not pray for the "world system," the cosmos that is opposed to God's will. He interceded for His people. That should give believers serene peace and confidence.

He prays, "Holy Father, keep through thine own name those whom thou hast given me, that they may be one, as we are" (v. 11*b*). The Lord emphasizes the Father's holiness. While He was on earth, the Lord kept them, and none is lost except the son of perdition (Judas, v. 12). Now the Lord is returning to the Father, and He is speaking these words that they might have "my joy fulfilled in them" (v. 13). Heaven is a place of joy, not sorrow. The Lord declares, "I have given them thy word; and the world hath hated them" (v. 14). Believers need to remember that the hatred of the world is evidence of God's favor. The Lord does not pray that the Father should "take them out of the world, but that thou shouldest keep them from the evil [one]" (v. 15). "They are not of the world, even as I am not of the world" (v. 16). Believers do not belong in the wicked world; they are just passing through it. Now He prays, "Sanctify them in [or *by*] thy truth; thy word is truth" (v. 17). This is one of the foundational passages for the doctrine of the verbal inspiration of the Scriptures. The Word of God does not merely contain the truth; it is truth. Anything that contradicts the Word of God is a lie. The Lord now sends believers into the world as witnesses to the truth (v. 18). He prays that they might be sanctified through the truth (v. 19). Receiving the truth of the Word of God (the Holy Bible) sets the believer apart for God and His service. God's people are Bible-believers. Those who deny the truth of the Bible are lost souls who need to repent and turn to the Lord Jesus Christ for salvation.

III. He Prays for Future Believers. vv. 20–26.

The Lord prays for those who will believe on Him through the disciples' ministry (v. 20). He prays for unity among them (v. 21). He certainly knows man's propensity toward divisions and arguments. He prays for glory upon them (v. 22). He prays that they may be made perfect in one that the world

---

17:11. The keeping power of God not only protects His people, but also gives them unity.

17:15. Only in eternity will believers understand how many times the Lord kept them from the evil one.

17:17. Note that the Lord does not say that the Word "may contain" the truth; He declares, "Thy word is truth." This is a divinely inspired endorsement of the Bible as pure truth by the Lord Jesus Christ Himself. He cannot be mistaken. See Custer, *Does Inspiration Demand Inerrancy?*; Young, Edward, *Thy Word Is Truth*; Lightner, Robert, *The Saviour and the Scripture*; Engelder, T. E., *Scripture Cannot Be Broken*; Warfield, Benjamin, *The Inspiration and Authority of the Bible.*

may know that the Father has sent Him (v. 23). He prays that His people may be with Him where He is and that they may behold His glory (v. 24). He knows that all these petitions will certainly be fulfilled by His loving heavenly Father. He concludes His prayer by praying, "O righteous Father, the world has not known thee: but I have known thee, and these have known that thou hast sent me" (v. 25). The world has distorted ideas about the nature of God, but the Lord knows His Father perfectly and completely (Aor.). He has "declared" to the disciples the Father's "name" (v. 26). The "name" is the characterization of God that embodies all the qualities of the divine nature (holiness, righteousness, wisdom, goodness, compassion, grace, love, mercy, longsuffering, etc.). The Lord's purpose in the prayer is "that the love wherewith thou hast loved me may be in them, and I in them" (v. 26). The divine Presence is to indwell the believer. It is the Spirit of God Who will impart spiritual understanding (I Cor. 2:10–14).

Practical Applications from John 17

1. Eternal life is knowing the true God and Jesus Christ the Savior (v. 3).
2. The great characteristic of the saints is that they have kept the Word of God (v. 6).
3. The Lord Jesus constantly prays (present tense) for His people (v. 9).
4. The great characteristics of God the Father are holiness (v. 11) and righteousness (v. 25).
5. The great instrument of sanctification is the Word of God (v. 17).
6. The Lord prays for all future believers and their unity (vv. 20–21).
7. The Lord prays that they all may be made perfect (v. 23).

Prayer

Dear Lord, thank You for loving us, dying for us, and praying for us. Help us to serve You forever. For Jesus' sake. Amen.

17:25–26. For a brief discussion of the attributes of God see Berkhof, *Systematic Theology*, pp. 52–81; for a more thorough treatment see Bavinck, Herman, *The Doctrine of God*, "Attributes," pp. 113–251.

17:26. For further discussion on prayer see *ZPEB*, "Prayer," IV, pp. 835–44; *ISBE*, "Prayer," III, pp. 931–39; *EDBT*, "Prayer," pp. 621–26; Murray, Andrew, *With Christ in the School of Prayer*, 274 pp.

JOHN 18

Gethsemane and the Trial

Persons

Jesus Christ
His disciples
Judas the betrayer
a band of men from the chief priests
Simon Peter
Malchus
Annas
Caiaphas
the woman doorkeeper
servants and officers of the high priest
the kinsman of the man whose ear Peter cut off
Pilate

Persons mentioned

the Jews
Barabbas

Places mentioned

the brook Cedron
a garden
the palace of the high priest
Pilate's judgment hall

Doctrines taught

the omniscience of Jesus
Jesus accepted the cup
One man should die for the people
No evil could be charged against Jesus
Jesus was a greater King

John 18 Exposition

I. Gethsemane and the Arrest. vv. 1–11.

After the prayer the Lord Jesus took His disciples over the brook Cedron into a garden. Judas also knew the place, for Jesus often took His disciples there (vv. 1–2). Judas led a band of men and officers from the chief priests and Pharisees, who came with torches and weapons (v. 3). The Lord Jesus, in full knowledge of what was going to happen, went forth and said, "Whom seek ye?" (v. 4). The men answer, "Jesus of Nazareth" (v. 5). The Lord responded, "I am." That was the name of Jehovah ("I am," Exod. 3:14). It was a name of divine majesty. When the Lord said that, the men went backwards and fell to the ground (v. 6). When He said, "Let these go their way" (v. 8), He was protecting the disciples as He had promised (17:12; 18:9). Peter then drew a sword and smote the high priest's servant, Malchus, cutting off his right ear (v. 10). Jesus healed the ear (Luke 22:51) and told Peter to put up his sword (v. 11). The officers of the Jews bound Jesus and led Him away to Annas first, and then to Caiaphas (v. 13). Caiaphas was the one who counseled that one man should die for the people (11:49–51; 18:14).

II. Peter's Denial. vv. 15–27.

Peter and John followed Jesus into the palace of the high priest (v. 15). John was known by the woman who watched the door, so she asked Peter

---

18:1. The other Gospels call the garden Gethsemane. See *ZPEB*, "Gethsemane," II, pp. 706–9; *ISBE*, "Gethsemane," II, pp. 457–58; John McRay, *Archaeology and the New Testament*, pp. 198–99. John uses an old word for *garden* (*kepos*, from Homer on) here and in John 18:26; 19:41. Elsewhere Luke alone uses it (Luke 13:19).

18:3. The word *band* is the word *speira*, which was the technical word for a cohort of Roman troops. It was a troop of Roman soldiers who arrested the Lord Jesus as Bruce notes (*John*, p. 340).

18:10. Why does John mention the name of Malchus? He may have converted later and become a member of the church. For Malchus see *ISBE*, "Malchus," III, p. 229; Harrison, R. K., ed., *The New Unger's Bible Dictionary*, "Malchus," p. 807.

18:11. The *cup* referred to the lot in life that God gave the person. It could be a cup of blessing for the righteous or a cup of punishment for the wicked. Here it is a cup of suffering for the Lord. See *ZPEB*, "Cup," I, pp. 1044–45; *ISBE*, "Cup," I, pp. 836–37

18:13. On the high priests see *ZPEB*, "Annas," I, p. 170; "Caiaphas," I, pp. 683–85; *ISBE*, "Annas," I, p. 128; "Caiaphas," I, pp. 570–71.

18:15–16. "Another disciple" is John's quiet way of mentioning that he was there. It is

whether he was a disciple also, and Peter denied (v. 17). Peter stood with the servants and officers, warming himself at the coals. The high priest asked Jesus of His disciples and doctrine (v. 19). Jesus answered that He had spoken openly to the world and not in secret, and asked why the high priest did not ask witnesses (vv. 20–21). One of the officers struck Jesus, saying, "Answerest thou the high priest so?" (v. 22). Jesus answered, "If I have spoken evil, bear witness of the evil: but if well, why smitest thou me?" (v. 23). As Peter stood and warmed himself by the coals, others asked him, "Art not thou also one of his disciples?" (v. 25). He replied, "I am not." A kinsman of the person whose ear Peter had cut off asked "Did not I see thee in the garden with him?" (v. 26). "Peter then denied again: and immediately the cock crew" (v. 27). The boldest of the apostles failed Him, just as Jesus had warned (13:38).

III. Pilate's Judgment Hall. vv. 28–40.

The Jews did not enter the judgment hall itself because doing so would make them ceremonially unclean, and hence unable to eat the Passover. F. F. Bruce comments, "There is, of course, characteristic Johannine irony in this reference to the chief priests' scrupulousness in the matter of ceremonial defilement, when all the time they were incurring incomparably greater moral defilement by their proceedings against Jesus" (*The Gospel of John*, p. 349). So Pilate went out and asked for their accusations against the Lord Jesus (v. 29). They respond ambiguously, "If He were not a malefactor, we would not have delivered him up unto thee" (v. 30). Thus they beg the question and give only vague accusations. Pilate perceives their answer correctly and commands them to judge Him according to their religious

---

not surprising that the high priest's doorkeeper would know a source of select fish for his dinners. See also John 20:2, 3, 4, 8.

18:17. The doorkeeper was a sharp-eyed woman who was responsible to keep out enemies and admit friends to the palace. See *ZPEB*, "Doorkeeper," II, p. 156; *ISBE*, "Gatekeeper; Doorkeeper," II, pp. 409–10.

18:18. The *fire* was a brazier of glowing coals.

18:22. It is typical that one of the officers struck Jesus with the palm of his hand. He was obviously used to roughing up prisoners before a trial. The Lord Jesus answered him very civilly.

18:28. The "hall of judgment" was in Pilate's palace. These Jews who would not go in were afraid of ceremonial defilement but were not afraid of murdering an innocent man.

law (v. 31). But they were seeking the death penalty, which needed Pilate's approval. Pilate returned to the judgment hall and asked the Lord Jesus, "Art thou the King of the Jews?" (v. 33). A king who was a rival of Caesar he could execute. The Lord asked him, "Sayest thou this thing of thyself, or did others tell it thee of me?" (v. 34). The Lord was clearly asking what evidence Pilate had for such a charge. In frustration Pilate asked, "What hast thou done?" (v. 35). The Lord answered, "My kingdom is not of this world: if my kingdom were of this world, then would my servants fight, that I should not be delivered to the Jews: but now is my kingdom not from hence" (v. 36). Pilate asked specifically, "Art thou a king then?" (v. 37). The Lord answered, "Thou sayest that I am a king"—in effect, "Your question shows that I am." The Lord goes on to claim that He bears witness to the truth. The politically wily Pilate asks, "What is truth?" (v. 38). He was prepared to use any lie to keep himself in office. He went out to the Jews and declared, "I find in him no fault," no cause for execution. He quickly adds, "Will ye therefore that I release unto you the King of the Jews?" But they all cry, "Not this man, but Barabbas" (v. 40) a "robber." This word translated *robber* does not denote a sneak thief but rather an armed and dangerous bandit, a man prepared to say, "Your money or your life!" Luke adds the note that Barabbas was a murderer (Luke 23:19).

Practical Applications from John 18

1. Jesus and His disciples regularly prayed in the Garden of Gethsemane (v. 2).
2. Jesus was prepared to drink the cup of persecution that His Father gave Him (v. 11).
3. Jesus did not deny that He was King of the Jews, but Peter denied Him and was very sorry (vv. 17–37).

18:31–33; 37–38. The famous "St. John Fragment" (Rylands Library Papyrus P52) is a manuscript fragment that has these verses on its two sides. It is dated before AD 100, and is the earliest copy of a New Testament document now in existence. For a beautiful photograph see Currie and Hyslop, *The Letter and the Scroll*, p. 311, a National Geographic book.

18:40. For Barabbas see *ZPEB*, "Barabbas," I, pp. 471–72; *ISBE*, "Barabbas," I, p. 429; Harrison, R. K., ed., *The New Unger's Bible Dictionary*, "Barabbas," p. 145.

18:37–40. For the OT doctrine of the king of the Jews see I Sam. 8:22; 10:24; Ps. 2:6; but behind all that, the Lord Jesus is the true, eternal King (Ps. 2:6; 10:16; 24:8).

4. Pilate was skeptical about knowing the truth, but he knows it now and is very sorry that he spurned it then (v. 38).
5. Barabbas, a bandit, was preferred before the Lord Jesus Christ (v. 40).

Prayer

Dear Lord, thank You, dear Savior, for taking our punishment and giving us life eternal instead. We praise You for infinite love and kindness that we can never deserve. Help us to reach out in love toward others. For Jesus' sake. Amen.

JOHN 19

The Crucifixion and Entombment

Persons

Pilate
Jesus
soldiers
chief priests and officers
the Jews
Mary, mother of Jesus
Mary, wife of Cleophas
Mary Magdalene
the disciple John
Joseph of Arimathea
Nicodemus

Persons mentioned

Caesar
two other men crucified also
Cleophas

Places mentioned

the judgment hall
the judgment seat, Gabbatha
Golgotha, the place of the skull
the Garden

Doctrines taught

Jesus was King of the Jews: the title on the cross said so
His death fulfilled Scripture (v. 37)
Nicodemus gave Him the burial of a King (100 pounds of spices, v. 39)

John 19 Exposition

I. The Condemnation by Pilate. vv. 1–16.

Pilate had the Lord Jesus scourged (v. 1). The soldiers wove a crown of thorns and put it on His head, and put on Him a purple robe (which was probably a scarlet centurion's robe, bleached purple by the sun). They cried out, "Hail, King of the Jews," and struck Him with their hands (v. 3). Pilate went out and repeated that he had found no fault in Him at all (v. 4). They bring out the Lord Jesus, wearing the crown of thorns and the purple robe, and Pilate says, "Behold the man!" (v. 5). The chief priests cried out, "Crucify him" (v. 6). Pilate said clearly, "I find no fault in him" (v. 6*b*). The Jews cried out, "By our law he ought to die, because he made himself the Son of God" (v. 7*b*). Pilate was afraid when he heard that, and went into the judgment hall and said to Jesus, "Whence art thou?" (v. 9). The Lord did not answer him. Pilate was irritated by the Lord's silence, but the Lord reminded Pilate that he had only delegated authority (v. 11). Pilate brought the Lord forth to the "Pavement" and said to the Jews, "Behold your King!" (vv. 13–14). The chief priests answered, "We have no king but Caesar" (v. 15). Pilate gave up and delivered Him to be crucified (v. 16). Pilate had a conscience, but no character.

II. The Crucifixion of Jesus. vv. 17–30.

They bring Jesus to the place of the skull, called Golgotha (skull) in Hebrew. It was by a well-traveled road (Matt. 27:39). They crucify the Lord

---

19:1. For the scourge see *ZPEB*, "Scourge," V, pp. 297–98; *ISBE*, "Scourge," IV, pp. 358–59.

19:2. There are two different species of thorn bushes (6–8 feet tall) that could have been used. There are several thorn bushes native to Palestine that have thorns 4 to 5 inches long. When such a "crown" was jammed on His head, it would draw blood. For discussion see *ZPEB*, "Crown of Thorns," I, p. 1040; *ISBE*, "Crown of Thorns," I, p. 832; Harrison, E. F., ed., *Baker's Dictionary of Theology*, "Crown," pp. 152–53.

19:5. Pilate cries out: "Behold the man"; contrast John the Baptist: "Behold the Lamb of God" (1:29). The world can see only a mere man.

19:13. The Gabbatha, also called "the Pavement," was an area of large stone slabs, over a yard square each, from which Pilate delivered his decision of condemnation of the Lord. It has been partially excavated. See *ZPEB*, "Gabbatha," II, p. 618; *ISBE*, "Gabbatha," II, p. 373.

19:14. "The sixth hour" is balanced against the "third hour," Mark 15:25. Roman reckoning and Jewish reckoning were different. See Westcott, *John*, pp. 282.

19:17. For Golgotha see *ZPEB*, "Golgotha," II, pp. 772–74; *ISBE*, "Golgotha," II, pp. 523–24.

between two obvious criminals to make it look like He belonged there. Pilate wrote a title for the cross: "Jesus of Nazareth the King of the Jews" (v. 19). The title was written in Hebrew, Greek, and Latin (v. 20). Jerusalem was a multilingual community. The chief priests asked Pilate to change the title to read that Jesus claimed that (v. 21), but he refused (v. 22). The soldiers divided His clothing among them and cast lots for His robe (vv. 23–24). This casting of lots fulfilled the prophecy of Psalm 22:18. The three Marys stood by the cross: His mother, the wife of Cleophas, and Mary Magdalene (v. 25). The Lord Jesus committed His mother to the care of John (vv. 26–27). The Lord Jesus knew that one more prophecy needed to be fulfilled, and so said, "I thirst" (v. 28). David had prophesied, "In my thirst they gave me vinegar to drink" (Ps. 69:21*b*). When Jesus had received the vinegar, He said, "It has been finished!" (v. 30). Every prophecy of His suffering had been fulfilled. Now He bowed His head and released His spirit. To the Jews death by crucifixion represented a curse (Deut. 21:23), but God turned it into a means of salvation for all who will believe. The atoning sacrifice for the sins of the world had now been accomplished (see Heb. 9:28; 10:12). No wonder that Paul wrote, "But God forbid that I should glory, save in the cross of our Lord Jesus Christ, by whom the world is crucified unto me, and I unto the world" (Gal. 6:14).

III. The Burial of His Body. vv. 31–42.

Since the day was the preparation day for the Passover celebration, the Jews asked Pilate to order that the legs of the crucified men be broken to hurry up the deaths so that they would not be there on the Passover. The soldiers broke the legs of the two malefactors, but they saw that Jesus was already dead (v. 33). Just to make sure, one of the soldiers pierced His side with a spear, and blood and water flowed out (v. 34). This fulfilled the directions of the Passover sacrifice (Exod. 12:46). It also fulfilled the prophecy of the

---

19:24. For the casting of lots see *ZPEB*, "Lots," III, p. 988; *ISBE*, "Lots," III, pp. 172–73.

19:25. For the 3 Marys see *ISBE*, III, pp. 268–69; "Mary," #1, Mary Magdalene; "Mary," #6, the mother of Jesus, and #3, Mary the wife of Clopas. See also *ZPEB*, IV, pp. 104–6; "Mary," #5, #6; "Mary, Mother of Jesus," IV, pp. 106–12.

For Mary Magdalene compare Matt. 27:56; Mark 15:40; Luke 8:2; 24:10; John 20:1, 11, 16, 18.

19:31.For the Jews' preparation day (for the Passover) see *ZPEB*, "Preparation Day," IV, p. 848; *ISBE*, "Preparation, Day of," III, pp. 953–54.

Messiah, "They shall look on him whom they pierced" (v. 37; Zech. 12:10). After this Joseph of Arimathea asked Pilate for the body of Jesus, and Pilate gave him permission (v. 38). Nicodemus came with a hundred pounds of myrrh and aloes (v. 39), a burial fit for a King, and the two of them wrapped the body of Jesus with the linen clothes and the spices (v. 40). They put the body in a new tomb in a garden that was near (vv. 41–42). They were borrowing the tomb just for the Passover weekend.

Practical Applications from John 19

1. The soldiers meant the term "King of the Jews" to be mockery, but they spoke the truth unwittingly (v. 3).
2. Pilate feared the people more than he feared God (vv. 15–16).
3. The soldiers did not realize that what they were doing was fulfilling Scripture (vv. 23–24).
4. We note Jesus' provision of care for His mother (vv. 26–27).
5. Myrrh and aloes were very expensive spices; Nicodemus was giving his very best to the Master (vv. 39–40).
6. It is significant that it was a borrowed tomb; the Lord did not need a permanent one.

Prayer

Dear Lord, help us to understand the enormity of what You have done in our behalf. It is easy to think of a man sacrificing himself for his God; but to think of the Great God sacrificing His dear Son on our behalf is beyond us. Thank You, Lord, for such infinite love and grace. Help us to let that love flow out to others. For Jesus' sake. Amen.

JOHN 20

The Resurrection of the Lord Jesus

Persons

Mary Magdalene
Simon Peter
the other disciple [John]
two angels
Jesus
My Father, My God
the disciples
Thomas Didymus

Persons mentioned

the disciples
ye (the reader addressed, v. 31)

Places mentioned

the sepulcher
the Upper Room

Doctrines taught

faith (v. 8)
the necessity of knowing Scripture
the reality of angels
Jesus' benediction of peace
the Ascension
the impartation of the Holy Spirit
the reality of the resurrection body
the Lordship of Christ
Christ did many other signs, which are not recorded in Scripture
Life comes through believing in Christ, the Son of God

John 20 Exposition

I. The Discovery of the Resurrection. vv. 1–10.

Mary Magdalene came early and saw the stone rolled away (v. 1). She told Peter and John that they have taken the Lord out of the sepulcher (v. 2). They run to the sepulcher. John gets there first and sees (present tense, "keeps on looking") the linen clothes lying, but he did not go in (v. 5). Then Peter arrives and goes into the tomb and sees (present tense) the linen clothes lying, and the cloth that had wrapped the head still in a wrapped condition, but collapsed flat (vv. 6–7). Then John went in, and he saw, and believed (v. 8). He understood that the Lord had risen through the clothes and left them behind. They did not yet remember or understand the Scripture that said He must rise again from the dead (v. 9; Ps. 16:10). The disciples then went away to their own homes (v. 10).

II. The Revelation to Mary Magdalene. vv. 11–18.

Mary stood outside the tomb weeping, and looked into the sepulcher, and saw two angels in white sitting where the body of Jesus had lain (vv. 11–12). They ask her, "Woman, why weepest thou?" She responds, "Because they have taken away my Lord, and I know not where they have laid him" (v. 13). She does not seem to grasp that they might know what happened. Then she turned back and saw Jesus standing there but did not recognize Him (v. 14). Jesus says to her, "Woman, why are you weeping; whom are you seeking?" (v. 15). She, supposing Him to be the gardener, says to Him, "Sir, if you carried him off, tell me where you laid him, and I will take him up." Jesus says to her, "Mary." "She turned herself and says to him in Hebrew, 'My rabbi' (which is saying, 'Teacher')" (v. 16, lit.). Jesus says to her, "Touch me not, for I have not yet ascended to my Father; but go to my brethren, and say to them, I am ascending to my Father, and your Father, and to my

---

20:1. The stone was a large disk of stone with one flat spot on the edge. When that flat spot was down, it would take some very strong men to move the stone away. The parallel passage in Matt. 28:2 declares that the angel of the Lord rolled the stone from the door and sat upon it. There was no stone that He could not move.

20:2. The reference to "the other disciple, whom Jesus loved" is a reference to the apostle John. Note John 13:23. See *ZPEB*, "John, the Apostle," III, pp. 637–41; *ISBE*, "John the Apostle," II, pp. 1107–8; Bruce, F. F., *The Gospel of John*, pp. 1–6.

20:15. The word *gardener* (*kepouros*) occurs only here in the Greek NT. The cognate word *garden* is in John 18:1, 26; 19:41.

God, and your God" (v. 17). Mary Magdalene comes and announces to the disciples, "I have seen the Lord," and He said these things to her (v. 18). Now she understood clearly what had happened.

III. The Revelation to the Eleven Disciples. vv. 19–29.

"Therefore the same day that evening, being the first day of the week, and the doors having been shut where the disciples were on account of fear of the Jews, Jesus came and stood in the midst, and says to them: Peace to you" (v. 19). Note John 14:27 also. The Lord then showed them His hands and His side; then the disciples were glad when they were sure that it was the Lord (v. 20). The Lord repeated His benediction of peace upon them and then sent them on a mission for Him. He breathed on them and said, "Receive ye the Holy Ghost: whose soever sins ye remit, they are remitted unto them; whose soever sins ye retain, they are retained" (vv. 22*b*–23). The Holy Spirit was going to empower their ministries. But Thomas was not with them when Jesus came (v. 24). The other disciples told Thomas about the Lord's victory, but he doubted their testimonies (v. 25). He boldly declared that he wanted to put his fingers into the print of the nails before he would believe. After eight days the disciples were together again with Thomas, the doors being shut (v. 26). The Lord Jesus stood in their midst, the doors being shut, and said, "Peace be unto you." He then addressed Thomas, "Reach hither thy finger, and behold my hands; and reach hither thy hand, and thrust it into my side; and be not faithless, but believing" (v. 27). Thomas said to Him, "My Lord and my God" (v. 28). There was absolutely no doubt left. Thomas gives one of the New Testament's most important confessions of the deity of Christ. There could be no doubt about the reality of Christ in His power and deity. The Lord pronounces a blessing on those who have not seen all that the apostles had, and yet have believed (v. 29).

20:20. There were healed scars where the gaping wounds had been.

20:28. The deity of Christ is one of the most important doctrines confessed by believers:

I. Thomas called Him "My Lord and my God" 20:28.

II. He is eternal: "In the beginning was the Word" (1:1).

III. He is Immanuel, "God with us" (Matt. 1:22–23; Isa. 7:13–14).

IV. He is "Lord of all" (Acts 10:36).

V. He is "our great God and Savior Jesus Christ" (Titus 2:13).

IV. The Revelation of the Purpose of John's Gospel. vv. 30–31.

The Lord Jesus did much more than just the miracles and signs recorded in John's Gospel. But John recorded these things in order that the reader might believe that Jesus is the Messiah, the Son of God, and that through believing might have eternal life through His name [Person]. John had an evangelistic purpose in writing his Gospel. To this day the Gospel of John is the primary instrument in leading an inquirer to faith in the Lord Jesus Christ. And so, dear reader, we appeal to you. If you have not received the Lord Jesus Christ as your Savior from sin, will you do so now? He alone can forgive your sins and make you a saint who can serve Him forever.

Practical Applications from John 20

1. Those who loved the Lord much came early to mourn (vv. 1–8).
2. Seeking Jesus is the most important thing for disciples to do (vv. 1ff.).
3. Mary was enabled to see the angels; they had been there all along (v. 12).
4. The disciples assembled together even though the Lord was gone (v. 19). We still do. The church is not an accident.

VI. He is immutable: "Jesus Christ the same yesterday, and today, and forever" (Heb. 13:8).

VII. He is "Jesus Christ, the faithful witness, the first begotten from the dead, and the ruler of the kings of the earth" (Rev. 1:5).

VIII. "In him dwelleth all the fullness of the Godhead bodily" (Col. 2:9).

IX. Only One Who was God would refer to God the Father and Himself by saying, "*We* will come unto him, and make *our* abode with him" (14:23).

See also Torrey, R. A., *What the Bible Teaches*, "About Christ," pp. 80–84; *ISBE*, "Person of Christ," III, pp. 781–801; *ZPEB*, "Christology," I, pp. 805–9; *EDBT*, "Christ, Christology," pp. 83–89; *NDBT*, "Jesus Christ," pp. 592–602; Edersheim, Alfred, *The Life and Times of Jesus the Messiah*, 2 vols.; Walvoord, John, *Jesus Christ Our Lord*, 318 pp.

Faith in the Lord Jesus Christ is a necessity for salvation. See Harrison, E. F., ed., *Baker's Dictionary of Theology*, "Faith," pp. 208–11; *ZPEB*, "Faith, Faithfulness," II, pp. 479–91; *ISBE*, "Faith," II, pp. 270–73; *EDBT*, "Faith," pp. 236–39.

20:30–31. Soul winners love to use John's Gospel in leading a person to faith in the Lord Jesus Christ. John clearly had this in mind as he wrote. R. A. Torrey gave a solemn warning to skeptics: "Denying the fact of the Deity of Jesus Christ does not make it any less a fact, but it does make the denier guilty of awful blasphemous slander." (*What the Bible Teaches*, p. 84).

5. The church receives spiritual power and authority by the presence of the Holy Spirit (vv. 22–23).
6. John wrote his Gospel with the express purpose of bringing people to faith in the Lord Jesus (vv. 30–31).

Prayer

Dear Lord, help us to seek You spiritually from the heart. Help us to make You the center of our lives and thoughts. Give us the zeal to serve You with all of our being. Help us to accomplish all Your will for our lives. For Jesus' sake. Amen.

JOHN 21

Teaching the Apostles to Follow Jesus

Persons

Jesus
Simon Peter
Thomas
Nathanael
James and John, sons of Zebedee

Persons mentioned

two unnamed disciples
Jonas, Peter's father

Places mentioned

the Sea of Tiberias
the world

Doctrines taught

The Lord Jesus determines the success of man's labors
The Lord restores the penitent
The Lord determines the lives of His followers
The Lord Jesus did much more than just the miracles recorded in Scripture

John 21 Exposition

I. The Lord Reveals Himself to the Disciples at the Sea of Galilee. vv. 1–14.

There were seven disciples gathered together, and Peter declared, "I am going to fish" (vv. 1–3). The other disciples agree to go with him (v. 3). That night they caught nothing (v. 3*b*). When morning broke, Jesus stood on the shore, but the disciples did not recognize Him (v. 4). Jesus therefore says to them, "Children, are you having anything to eat?" (v. 5*a*). They answered Him, "No." But He said to them: "Cast the net on the right side of the boat, and you shall find" (v. 6*a*). They assumed that He might be able to see from the shore a school of fish that they could not see. They did cast, therefore, and they were not strong enough to draw the net in from "the multitude of the fishes" (v. 6*b*). John (the disciple whom Jesus loved) said to Peter, "It is the Lord." Peter jumped in and swam to shore to see the Lord (v. 7). The rest of the disciples came to shore dragging the net full of fish (v. 11). The disciples saw a fire of coals burning there, and fish roasting on it and bread. Although the net turned out to have 153 fish caught in it, the net did not break (vv. 9–11). The Lord invited the disciples, "Come and eat breakfast" (v. 12). None of them dared to ask Him Who He was, "knowing that it was the Lord" (v. 12). The Lord Jesus gave them the bread and the fish (v. 13). John notes that this was the third time that the Lord showed Himself to the disciples after His Resurrection (v. 14).

21:1. The Sea of Galilee was often called the Sea of Tiberias after the name of the most important city on the western shore. To this day it remains such. It was named in honor of the emperor Tiberius. See *ZPEB*, "Tiberias," V, pp. 746–47; *ISBE*, "Tiberias," IV, pp. 846–47; For color photos see Custer, *Stones of Witness*, pp. 41, 48–51.

21:2. It is not surprising that so many of the disciples were fishermen. Fishing was, and is, a major industry along the shores of Galilee. Tilapia is still the major variety of fish sold along the shores of Galilee. See *ZPEB*, "Fish, Fishing," II, pp. 541–44; *ISBE*, "Fish," "Fishing," II, pp. 308–11; Butler, Trent, ed., *Holman Bible Dictionary*, "Fish, Fishing," pp. 494–96, with color photos.

21:8. John identifies the vessel as a "little boat." The diminutive underscores the fact that the disciples were poor fishermen with humble equipment.

21:11. Fishermen like Peter and John would have thought to count the catch of the day. John remarked, "Yet the net was not broken." He was used to mending breaks in the net from a much smaller catch.

II. The Lord Restores Peter. vv. 15–19.

The Lord asked Peter, "Simon, son of John, are you loving me (with a high and holy love, *agapao*) more than these?" (v. 15). Peter had boasted that though all others would be offended, yet he would not be (Mark 14:29). Now Peter does not dare make such claims, but says merely, "Thou knowest that I am affectionate toward thee" (*phileo*). The Lord then asks, "Are you loving me (with this high and holy love)?" (v. 16). Peter did not dare use that word; he said again, "I am affectionate toward thee" (*phileo*). The Lord said, "Shepherd my lambs" (v. 16*b*). The third time Jesus asked, "Simon, son of John, are you affectionate toward me?" (v. 17). Here He chose Peter's word, and that broke Peter's heart. There was no boasting left. He answered, "Lord, Thou knowest that I am affectionate toward thee" (v. 17*b*). The Lord responded, "Keep feeding my sheep" (v. 17*b*). Every pastor needs to remember that he is just as weak as the weakest member of his flock and that he needs the Lord's sustaining grace just as much. The Lord goes on to warn Peter that he was self-confident when he was young, but when he would be old, he would be carried to a martyr's death (vv. 18–19*a*). He had to depend on the sustaining grace of the Lord Jesus, just as all believers must. And then the Lord commands, "Keep on following me" (v. 19*b*). Every believer must follow this admonition. We must all keep on following the Lord, wherever He leads.

III. The Lord Has an Individual Will for Each Believer. vv. 20–25.

Peter sees John following and asks, "What shall this man do?" (v. 21). Peter was wondering if the Lord was "playing favorites"! The Lord tells Peter

---

21:15. The word *lamb* occurs in John's Gospel only here. The word moves Christian workers to reach out to young converts to strengthen them in their service and testimony for the Lord.

21:15–17. It was vitally important that Peter be restored from his denial of the Lord (18:15–27). He had denied the Lord three times; now he must confess the Lord three times. He never wavered again (Acts 2:14, 38; 4:8–19; 8:20; 9:34–40; 12:3–18).

Only eternity will reveal the impact that John's Gospel has had on the conversion and consecration of God's servants. For further study of the Gospel of John see *ZPEB*, "John, Gospel of," III, pp. 657–74; *ISBE*, "John, Gospel According to," II, pp. 1098–1107; *EDBT*, "John, Theology of," pp. 423–27; *NDBT*, "John," pp. 280–85; Bruce, F. F., *The Gospel of John*, 425 pp.; Westcott, B. F., *The Gospel According to John*, 307, 97 pp.; Godet, F., *Commentary on the Gospel of John*, 2 vols. 559, 551 pp. See also the bibliography for more extensive studies.

what all believers need to remember. The Lord has a special will for every believer, and none should envy or desire the Lord's perfect will for others. Whatever it may be, the Lord's will for every believer is perfect. Although some thought that the Lord meant John would not die, John explains that the Lord did not say that. The "we know" in verse 24 is a reference to the elders of John's church. They had great confidence in his careful testimony. John concludes with the statement that he has made no attempt to be exhaustive in his record of the Lord's life and ministry. He wrote what he was inspired to write. Plainly there was much, much more that he could have written. And so the ministry of writing about the Lord and His Word continues to this day.

Practical Applications from John 21

1. The Lord Jesus reveals Himself to His disciples; we do not accidentally "discover" Him (v. 1).
2. Self-effort counts for nothing in the Christian life (v. 3).
3. Following the direction of the Lord is the path of Christian success (v. 6).
4. The Lord Jesus had prepared for the disciples ahead of time (v. 9).
5. The Lord Jesus restored Peter after his denials (vv. 15–17).
6. In every case the Lord's directions concerned the sheep and lambs of His flock.
7. Every believer is to follow the Lord Jesus directly, without regard to others (vv. 21–22).
8. The revelation of the Lord Jesus Christ is vastly greater than what any book can record (v. 25).

Prayer

Dear Lord, help us to serve You from the heart, both in this realm and forever. For Jesus' sake. Amen.

ANNOTATED BIBLIOGRAPHY

Conservative Commentaries

Alford, Henry. John in vol. 1 of *The Greek Testament*. 4 vols. London: Rivingtons, 1871; reprinted. Moody, 2 vols. pp. 50–73, 677–924.

A thorough exposition of the Greek text. He defends John's authorship (pp. 50ff.); stresses that Christ was "very God" in the beginning (p. 681; holds that *Lamb of God* comes from Isa. 53:7 (p. 696); thinks that the Lord spoke John 3:16 (p. 718); terms chapters 14–17 the most holy place (p. 846).

Boice, James Montgomery. *The Gospel of John*. 4 vols. Grand Rapids: Zondervan, 1975. 443 pp.

He stresses that Jesus is God (vol. I, pp. 21ff.) and Man (pp. 29ff.); attacks the idea of the universal fatherhood of God and brotherhood of man (p. 87); interprets "only begotten" as *unique* (p. 116); denies that Jesus was a revolutionary (pp. 205ff.).

Bonar, Horatius. *Studies in the Gospel of John*. 1869; rpt. Grand Rapids: Zondervan, 1972. 110 pp.

Fervent devotional messages. He warns against seeing Jesus merely as a teacher instead of a Savior (pp. 15–18); defends the doctrine of the Trinity (pp. 54f.).

Borchert, Gerald L. *John 1–11; 12–21*. 2 vols. Nashville: Broadman & Holman, 1996.

One of the best recent expositions. He rejects the form-critical views of Bultmann (p. 34); defends Johannine authorship, but with an amanuensis (pp. 81–91); attacks the interpretations of Jehovah's Witnesses (p. 103); holds that Jesus made real wine in Cana (p. 157); argues that Jesus used "I am" as a theophany (p. 259); gives personal experiences with the sheep in Israel (p. 330).

Brown, David. *John*. In vol. 5 of A *Commentary Critical, Experimental, and Practical*, ed. Jamieson, Fausset, and Brown. 1869; rpt. Grand Rapids: Eerdmans, 1945. pp. 346–486.

A conservative exposition. He stresses the deity and humanity of Christ (pp. 346, 48); and His absolute knowledge (p. 361); stresses the divine personality of the Spirit (pp. 448f.); lists the 7 words from the cross (pp. 470–74); calls John's Gospel the "Sun of the Scripture" (p. 486).

Bruce, Frederick Fyvie. *The Gospel of John*. Grand Rapids: Eerdmans, 1983. 425 pp.

A very helpful exposition of the Greek text of John. He defends John the son of Zebedee as author (pp. 1ff.); also defends the eternal preexistence of the Word and His identity as the divine Son (pp. 31, 45); argues that Jesus used language that only God could use (p. 206); holds that "the Johannine Jesus is always praying, for he and the Father are one" (p. 248).

Calvin, John. *Commentary on the Gospel According to John*. 2 vols. 1553; rpt. Grand Rapids: Eerdmans, 1949. 2 vols. 457, 346 pp.

A classic Reformed exposition. He stresses the eternal divinity of Christ (I, p. 25); attacks the "Papists" (I, pp. 41, 73, 75, etc.); stresses the two natures of Christ as God and Man (I, p. 46); stresses that God elects those who are saved (I, p. 252); warns of the dreadful judgment of God on the reprobate (II, p. 42).

Chrysostom, John. *Homilies on the Gospel of St. John*. In vol. 14 of *The Nicene and Post-Nicene Fathers*, ed. Philip Schaff. Grand Rapids: Eerdmans, 1956, rpt. 334 pp.

Comfort, Philip Wesley. *I Am the Way: A Spiritual Journey Through the Gospel of John*. Grand Rapids: Baker Books, 1994. 212 pp.

A warmly devotional exposition of John. He stresses the journey motif that organizes the Gospel (pp. 15–31); notes that John the Baptist is the first to the way (p. 42); sees Exodus imagery in John 6 (p. 69); shows that Jesus was the way to the Father (pp. 119ff.).

Darby, J. N. *Notes on the Gospel of John*. London: Morrish, n.d. 288 pp.

Expositions by a famous leader of the Plymouth Brethren. He stresses the deity of the Lord Jesus (pp. 1ff.); gives unequal expositions (2 pages on John 2, but 32 pp. on John 3).

Dods, Marcus. "The Gospel of St. John." In Vol. 1 of *The Expositor's Greek Testament*. 1909; rpt. Grand Rapids: Eerdmans, n.d., pp. 655–872.

He claims that in John we "have the direct testimony of an eyewitness" (p. 655); John provides unique details: "the hour at which Jesus sat on the well, the number and size of the water-pots at the marriage at Cana, the weight and value of the ointment, the number of fish at the last cast, the hour at which the nobleman's son began to amend, the hour at which Jesus took the two inquirers into his own lodging" (p. 669).

Erdman, Charles R. *The Gospel of John*. Philadelphia: Westminster, 1916. 178 pp.

A brief, conservative exposition. He stresses that Jesus is the divine, unique Son of God (p. 8); suggests that the three great ideas of John are testimony, faith, and life (p. 23).

Gaebelein, Arno Clemens. *The Gospel of John*. New York: "Our Hope" Publications, 1936. 414 pp.

An exposition by a well-known Fundamentalist. He defends the deity of Christ (p. 11), His sinlessness (p. 23), His bodily resurrection (p. 381); he attacks Unitarianism, Christian Science, Russellism, modernists, Romanists. He regards John 17 as the most precious portion of the Gospel (p. 311).

Godet, F. *Commentary on the Gospel of John*. 2 vols. New York: Funk & Wagnalls, 1886. 559, 551 pp.

He holds that the ruling idea of John is the incarnate Logos (Vol. I, p. 66); defends Johannine authorship (I, pp. 167–204); argues that Jesus as the Lamb of God fulfills the type of the Servant of Jehovah in Isa. 53 (I, p. 312); stresses the eyewitness nature of John's description of the raising of Lazarus (II, p. 190); calls John 17 the prayer of the High Priest of mankind, "who begins his sacrifice by offering Himself to God" (II, p. 323).

Gutzke, Manford George. *Plain Talk on John*. Grand Rapids: Zondervan, 1968. 213 pp.

Devotional and practical messages. He calls Christ the eternal Son of God (p. 12).

Harrison, Paul W. *The Light That Lighteth Every Man*. Grand Rapids: Eerdmans, 1958. 329 pp.

Devotional studies by a former missionary to Arabia. He defends the humanity and divinity of Jesus (p. 18); interprets passages in the light of present day Arabian customs (p. 39); emphasizes the iron legalism of the Pharisees (pp. 154f., 169); warns against human religious zeal (p. 205).

Kent, Homer A., Jr. *Light in the Darkness*. Grand Rapids: Baker, 1974. 239 pp.

Brief paragraph expositions. He defends Johannine authorship (pp. 14–22); includes a number of photographs to illustrate the text (pp. 30, 51, 57, 71, 73, 87, etc.); defends the deity of Christ (pp. 91, 129).

Lange, John Peter. *John*. Lange's Commentary on the Holy Scriptures, ed. Philip Schaff, 1871; rpt. Grand Rapids: Zondervan, n.d. 654 pp.

A conservative Lutheran commentary. He defends the genuineness (pp. 24ff.); stresses the deity and humanity of Christ (p. 49); stresses the unity and inspiration of Scripture (p. 334); holds that the knowledge of God includes the knowledge of Christ (p. 514).

Laurin, Roy L. *John: Eternal Life*. Chicago: Moody, 1972. 287 pp.

A devotional commentary. He stresses the new birth (p.15), baptism by immersion (p. 27); attacks the doctrine of the fatherhood of God and brotherhood of man (p. 43); but he quotes liberals with approval: Tillich (p. 105), Buttrick (p. 208).

Lenski, Richard Charles Henry. *The Interpretation of St. John's Gospel*. Columbus, OH: Lutheran Book Concern, 1942. 1444 pp.

An exhaustive Lutheran commentary. He stresses the absolute deity and preexistence of Christ (pp. 33f, 671), His divine and human natures (pp. 72f.); holds that *only begotten* refers to the eternal generation of the Son, not merely the incarnation (pp. 77ff., 96f.); attacks immersion (pp. 117ff.); defends verbal inspiration and inerrancy of the Bible (pp. 130, 767); teaches a general resurrection and judgment (pp. 397f.); allows loss of salvation (p. 1038); holds that Jesus arose through the burial clothes, leaving them flat (pp. 134).

Luther, Martin. *Sermons on the Gospel of St. John*. Vols. 22–24 of *Luther's Works*. St. Louis: Concordia, 1957, 1959, 1961. 558, 448, 448 pp.

Sermons preached at different times from 1530–38 on John's Gospel. He defends the doctrine of the Trinity (22:5–6); attacks the infallibility of the pope (22:262); stresses that our faith is centered in Christ as God (24:97f.); stresses the office of the Holy Spirit in guiding preachers of the Word (24:362).

Macaulay, J. C. *Devotional Studies in St. John's Gospel*. Grand Rapids: Eerdmans, 1941. 285 pp.

He sets forth the eternity, personality, and deity of Christ (p. 17); gives a premillennial interpretation of the resurrection and judgment (pp. 77f., 121); stresses that the answer to the world's hatred is witness (p. 200); thinks that the graveclothes looked as though the body had evaporated (p. 268).

Maclaren, Alexander. *The Gospel of St. John*. Bible class expositions. 1893; rpt. Grand Rapids: Zondervan, 1960. 231 pp.

Brief expository studies. He stresses the eternal existence of the Word (p. 3); holds that the miracle at Cana manifested Christ as Creator and Sustainer (p. 23); terms the raising of Lazarus the "crowning miracle" (pp. 112f.); warns that the organized church may become the worst enemy of the true church (p. 159).

Meyer, Frederick Brotherton. *The Life and Light of Men: Love to the Uttermost*. 2 vols. 1898; rpt. New York: Revell, n.d. 251, 254 pp.

Warmly devotional expositions. He stresses the need of being born again (I, p. 73) maintains the Lord's consciousness of His deity (I, p. 108); defends the doctrine of the Trinity (II, pp. 59f.); calls John 17 "the most precious fragment of the past" (p. 142).

Michaels, J. Ramsey. *John*. New International Biblical Commentary. Peabody, MA: Hendrickson, 1989. 386 pp.

A conservative commentary based on the NIV. He holds that the deity of Christ is presupposed throughout the narrative (p. 25); defends "One and Only" as a translation of *monogenes* (p. 26); sees the connection between "Lamb" in John and Revelation (p. 35); stresses Jesus' use of "I am" (pp. 77, 154, 305); defends the miracle of walking on the water (p. 107).

Morgan, G. Campbell. *The Gospel According to John*. New York: Revell, n.d. 333 pp.

A careful exposition. He organizes the Gospel by the places and signs manifested (pp. 7–8); holds that we cannot account for the life of Jesus on the "ground of that which is purely natural" (p. 134); stresses that Christ claimed eternal existence (p. 161); gives an apt illustration of Christ the Door (p. 177); holds that the graveclothes had fallen flat rather than being unwound (pp. 309f.).

Morris, Leon. *The Gospel According to John*. Grand Rapids: Eerdmans, 1971. 936 pp.

A thorough defense and exposition of the Gospel. He defends the deity of Christ (p. 77); lists seven who witness to the Lord (p. 90); defends the reading "only begotten God" in 1:18 (p. 113); has additional notes on Logos (pp. 115ff.); defends the doctrine of the wrath of God (p. 249); stresses that Jesus claimed deity (pp. 466, 473); defends the Resurrection of Jesus (pp. 830ff.).

Reith, George. *The Gospel According to St. John.* 2 vols. Edinburgh: Clark, 1889. 197, 176 pp.

A warmly devotional exposition of John. He defines "only begotten" as showing Jesus Christ's eternal, necessary, and essential relation to the Father (I, 14); makes familiar verses glow (3:16, I, pp. 51–52); teaches the eternal co-existence of the Father and the Son (I, p. 84); the preexistence of the Son (II, p. 22); defends the doctrine of the Trinity (II, p. 114).

Ridderbos, Herman N. *The Gospel According to John.* Grand Rapids: Eerdmans, 1997. 721 pp.

A theological commentary. He argues that the evangelists are not just recording facts, but are seeking to bring readers to faith in Christ (p. 7); he defends the idea that the Word is God, not an attribute abstracted from God (p. 25); rejects Bultmann's Gnostic explanations (p. 31); holds that Jesus is the Lamb with God-given power and authority to take away the sins of the world (p. 74); urges that one must be born again "from above," rather than merely "again" (pp. 125–26); denies that "eating Christ" is sacramental language (p. 235); stresses that Jesus is the door through which the sheep enter the sheepfold (p. 357).

Robertson, Archibald Thomas. *Word Pictures in the New Testament, Vol. V: The Fourth Gospel and Hebrews.* Nashville: Broadman Press, 1932. pp. 1–323.

A careful and conservative exposition of the Greek text by a master grammarian.

Tasker, R. V. G. *The Gospel According to St. John.* Tyndale Commentaries. Grand Rapids: Eerdmans, 1960. 237 pp.

Brief conservative commentary. He defends Johannine authority, not authorship (pp. 11ff.); thinks that 7:53–8:11, though genuine, was not an original part of John (p. 110; stresses the Lord's divine nature and preexistence (p. 120); holds that the graveclothes were "still lying in their original folds, untouched by human hands yet no longer containing the crucified body" (p. 221).

Tenney, Merrill C. *John: The Gospel of Belief.* Grand Rapids: Eerdmans, 1948. 321 pp.

A study guide to John. He lists the 7 signs (pp. 30–31); gives a chart to show the divisions of John (pp. 40–41); holds that Christ is called "only begotten God" in 1:18 (p. 72); argues that Christ was deity (p. 168).

———. "John," in vol. 9 of *The Expositor's Bible Commentary*, ed. Frank E. Gaebelein. Grand Rapids: Zondervan, 1981. pp. 1–203.

Brief conservative exposition. He defends the unity and Johannine authorship (pp. 4–9); regards the central theme as "belief" (p. 12); holds that Logos is an expression of personality in communication (p. 28); thinks that 3:16 is John's comment (p. 49); argues that Jesus' statement *before Abraham I am* "could only mean a claim to deity" (p. 99); thinks Jesus was crucified on Friday (p. 135); calls crucifixion "the most diabolical form of death ever invented" (p. 181).

Turner, George A., and Julius R. Mantey. *The Gospel According to John*. Grand Rapids: Eerdmans, n.d. 420 pp.

An Arminian New Evangelical exposition. They commend Albert Schweitzer (p. 1) and E. Stanley Jones (p. 288). They defend John's authorship (pp. 1926); attack racial prejudice (p. 110); teach a general resurrection (p. 76) and the deity and humanity of Christ (pp. 139, 163, 195); they state that 7:53–8:11 is not part of the text (p. 188).

Van Ryn, August. *Meditations in John*. Chicago: Moody Press, 1949. 205 pp.

Brief devotional studies from John. He stresses that the theme of John is belief in Christ as the Son of God (pp. 11ff.); lists a number of "sevens" in John (pp. 16f.); discusses "I am—seven great claims" (pp. 43ff.).

Vine, W. E. *John: His Record of Christ*. London: Oliphants, 1948. 192 pp.

Brief expository notes. He stresses that Christ is Creator and Author of life (p. 9); sees the miracle at Cana as foreshadowing millennial glory (p. 19); stresses the two resurrections (p. 44); teaches the Rapture and the tribulation period (pp. 62, 128).

Westcott, Brooke Foss. *The Gospel According to St. John*. 1881; rpt. Grand Rapids: Eerdmans, 1964. 307 + 97 pp.

Still perhaps the best commentary on the Greek text of John. He defends Johannine authorship (pp. v–xxxii); stresses that the absolute, eternal, immanent relations of the Persons of the Godhead are the basis for the revelation of the Word (p. 2); holds that in Christ eternity and time, the divine and the human are reconciled (p. 10); stresses that God's enabling does not destroy man's freedom (p. 104); teaches Christ's timeless existence (p. 140); calls the raising of Lazarus a revelation of Christ's divine glory (p. 164); holds that the falling of the soldiers showed that the Lord chose to give Himself up to them (p. 258); defends the Johannine authorship of John 21 (p. 299).

Yarbrough, Robert W. *John*. Chicago: Moody Press, 1991. 216 pp.

A brief conservative commentary. He outlines the geographical movement in the Gospel (p. 16); stresses the necessity of the new birth (pp. 39f.); holds that Jesus claimed to be the "I am" of Exodus 3:14 (p. 96); stresses that Jesus is the true Shepherd opposed to the false shepherds of Israel (pp. 106ff.).

Yates, Kyle M. *Preaching from John's Gospel*. Nashville: Broadman, 1964. 181 pp.

Expository sermons from John. He stresses that Jesus is the eternal Son of God (p. 6); shows that the Son is equal to the Father (p. 58); holds that "I come again" includes Christ's Resurrection, His sending of the Spirit, and His second coming (p. 129); thinks that the graveclothes looked "as if he had evaporated from them, leaving no disturbance" (p. 168).

Critical Commentaries

Abbey, Merrill R. *Encounter with Christ*. New York: Abingdon, 1961. 176 pp.

Liberal sermons drawn from John. He calls Jesus' choice of the cross "pathetic" (p. 122); teaches theistic evolution (pp. 139f.).

Appleton, George. *John's Witness to Jesus*. New York: Association Press, 1955. 96 pp.

He thinks that the book was written by a disciple of John (p. 9); calls the early confessions of faith "outbursts of exalted hope" (p. 23); explains the falling down of Jesus' arresters as merely surprise at Jesus' courage (p. 79).

Barclay, William. *The Gospel of John*. 2 vols. Philadelphia: Westminster, 1955. 309, 338 pp.

A liberal exposition. He denies that Jesus is identical with God, but in Him we see what God is like (I, pp. 17, 56); does not think that Jesus could know the past of another (I, p. 140); stresses that in heaven there is room for all (II, p. 179).

Barrett, Charles Kingsley. *The Gospel According to St. John*. New York: Macmillan, n.d. 531 pp.

A thorough commentary on the Greek text; however, it is dry bones with little spiritual perception. He thinks that three different disciples of John wrote Revelation, the Epistles, and the Gospel and circulated them under his name (pp. 113ff.); thinks that "I am" is merely an affirmation; holds that the conversation between Jesus and Nicodemus is a dialogue between the church and synagogue (p. 169); thinks that John has contradictions in his narrative (p. 347); is not sure of the historical value of the Resurrection narrative in John (p. 466); does not think chapter 21 is by John (p. 480).

Beasley-Murray, George R. *John*. Vol. 36 of Word Biblical Commentary. Waco: Word Books, 1987. 441 pp.

He distinguishes the beloved disciple from John the Apostle (pp. lxx–lxxv); holds that "I am" is merely an affirmation of Jesus as the revelation of God (p. 139); denies that John 15–17 was uttered on the way from the Upper Room to Gethsemane (p. 223); has no comment on "Thy word is truth" (p. 300).

Bernard, J. H. *The Gospel According to St. John*. 2 vols. International Critical Commentary. New York: Scribner's. 1929. 928 pp.

He holds that John the Elder, not the Apostle, is the author (p. lxiv); does not think that John really said, "Behold the Lamb" (p. 46); holds that the brethren of Christ were sons of Joseph by a first wife (p. 86); wants to switch the order of John 5 and 6 (p. 171); wants to put John 14 after John 15 and 16 (pp. 477ff.); does not think that John 17 has the exact words of the Lord (p. 557); thinks that the falling to the ground means no more than that they recoiled in fear (p. 586).

Berkeley, James P. *Reading the Gospel of John*. Philadelphia: Judson, 1958. 290 pp.

A liberal interpretation which sometimes manifests clear insight into the Greek text. He rearranges the order of the Gospel to improve its meaning (p. 101); by his definition of Spirit he teaches Modalism (p. 268).

Brown, Raymond E. *John*. Vols. 29, 29A of *The Anchor Bible*. New York: Doubleday, 1966, 1970. 1354 pp.

A thorough liberal interpretation. He holds that the Gospel of John had several authors and editors (pp. lxxxviiff.); imagines that John the Baptist thought that Jesus was Elijah (p. 64); sees the hand of several authors in John 3 (p. 136); thinks that John 14–16 is not a unity (p. 582), and that John 17 was added by a later redactor (p. 745); holds that the falling of the soldiers was "a Johannine theological construction," not historical (p. 811); thinks that a redactor added John 21 (p. 1080).

Bultmann, Rudolf. *The Gospel of John: A Commentary*. Oxford: Blackwell, 1971. 744 pp.

A study in form-critical unbelief. He refers to the legend of the virgin birth (pp. 62–63), the myth of the coming Paraclete (p. 588); the mythological ideas of the ascension and parousia (p. 581); thinks that John 17 presents the prayer not of the "historical Jesus" but of the church community (p. 522); attacks the whole doctrine of the Resurrection of the Lord (pp. 687ff.).

Dodd, Charles Harold. *The Interpretation of the Fourth Gospel*. Cambridge: Cambridge University Press, 1953. 478 pp.

He holds that the language applied to the Lord is highly mythological (p. 294); imagines that the woman of Samaria symbolizes the syncretistic cults of Samaria (p. 313); holds that "I come again" does not refer to the Second Coming but to the union which eternal life will bring (p. 405); thinks that John carefully composed discourses to teach theology (p. 445).

Haenchen, Ernst. *John 1. Hermeneia*. Philadelphia: Fortress Press, 1984. 308 pp.

A hypercritical interpretation by a post-Bultmannian. He mentions the "disorder and rearrangement" of the Gospel of John (pp. 44f.); thinks that the author chose an older hymn for the Prologue (pp. 77, 101); denies that "Lamb of God" alludes to Isa. 53:7 (p. 153); thinks that the walking on water was an old story that had undergone more than one development (p. 281).

Howard, Wilbert F., and A. J. Gossip. *John* in vol. 8 of *The Interpreter's Bible*. New York: Abingdon, 1955. pp. 435–811.

They admit an early date, but think that the Gospel was mixed up in assembling the final copy (p. 442); they wish to change the term *God* to *divine* when applied to the Son (p. 479); they think that Christ healed by suggestion (p. 538); they prefer the view that there is room for all in the Father's house (p. 699); they hold that the teaching of Buddhism is worthy of being put alongside that of Christ (p. 765).

Lightfoot, R. H. *St. John's Gospel*. Oxford: Clarendon, 1956. 368 pp.

A liberal commentary. He interprets "only begotten" as unique (p. 86); argues against Dodd that John presents the Lord as the true Passover Lamb (pp. 349–56).

Lindars, Barnabas. *The Gospel of John*. New Century Bible. London: Oliphants, 1972. 648 pp.

Liberal comments on the RSV. He thinks that the modern reader will have difficulty with John's worldview (pp. 24–25); denies that the author was John the Apostle (p. 34); does not think that the miracle at Cana is historical (p. 124); thinks that the raising of Lazarus is "a fresh piece of creative writing" (p. 386).

McClymont, J. A. *St. John*. New Century Bible. New York: Frowde, n.d. 352 pp.

He does not think that Christ foresaw the apostasy of Judas (p. 189); holds that though Christ claimed preexistence, He did not know everything (pp. 212, 241); thinks that the promise "I will come again" refers to the Holy Spirit (p. 276).

MacGregor, G. H. C. *The Gospel of John*. New York: Harper, 1928. 446 pp.

A critical interpretation. He thinks that John was interested not in history but spiritual truth (p. xx); holds that the author was not John, but a follower of the beloved disciple, who in turn was a follower of John (p. xlviii); calls the miracle at Cana "unintelligible and purposeless" (p. 48); thinks the author was influenced by the mystery religions (p. 70); does not think that Christ really raised Lazarus (p. 253); denies the authenticity of John 21 (p. 367).

Richardson, Alan. *Gospel According to Saint John*. London: SCM Press, 1959. 220 pp.

A brief liberal commentary. He doubts the genuineness of the miracle at Cana; thinks that the raising of Lazarus gives a truth "by means of a story that is not literally true" (p. 137); denies the genuineness of the 153 fish (21:11).

Sanders, J. N., and B. A. Mastin. *The Gospel According to St. John*. Harper's Commentaries. New York: Harper & Row, 1968. 480 pp.

A liberal commentary. They think that John's theology differs from that of Jesus (p. 19); hold that the author was John Mark (pp. 50f.); they do not think that John the Baptist called Jesus the Lamb that takes away sin (p. 93); leave open the possibility that Lazarus was not really dead (p. 274); hold that John 21 was added later (p. 440).

Schnackenburg, Rudolf. *The Gospel According to St. John*. 3 vols. New York: Seabury Press, 1980. 638, 556, 672 pp.

Exhaustive comments by a Roman Catholic. He argues that John the Apostle was responsible for some material, the evangelist-writer put it all together, and other editors added more material (pp. 100–04); argues that being born of water and spirit means baptismal regeneration (pp. 369ff.).

Sloyan, Gerard S. *John*. Interpretation. Atlanta: John Knox Press, 1988. 239 pp.

He discusses the sources the first author employed, the editor of the second edition, and the genius of the final editor (p. 3); stresses that history is not the right measuring-rod to apply to religious works (p. 8); holds that John the Baptist's testimony is that Jesus is the Lamb of God Who will take away the world's burden of sin and adds "the Evangelist is sure of this and has no problem in making John say it" (p. 13); thinks that John 6 should come before John 5 (p. 61); argues that "it would be a mistake to see in 'I am' used absolutely (8:24, 28, 58), a claim to identification with God" (it comes more likely from cultic usage in early liturgies (p. 101); thinks that John 14–16 "may well have come as a reflection on the prayer of chapter 17" (p. 174).

Strachan, R. H. *The Fourth Gospel*. 3rd ed. London: SCM Press, 1941. 345 pp.

He admits that Jesus is portrayed in John as a divine-human person (pp. 4–5); thinks that John wrote the raising of Lazarus as an act of "creative artistry" (p. 29); denies Johannine authorship (p. 88); holds that Jesus' claim of "I am" means only that He will not share His place as Mediator with anyone (p. 217); holds that "I come again" refers to death and the coming Holy Spirit (p. 280).

Whitacre, Rodney A. *John*. Vol. 4 of IVP New Testament Commentary. Downers Grove: InterVarsity Press, 1999. 526 pp.

Concerning authorship he comments, "I will refer to John as the author not in the sense that he necessarily wrote it all, but in recognition that it is his witness that is presented here" (p. 21). He dates John in the early 90s (p. 26); holds that *monogenes* does not mean "only begotten" but that this sense is true of Jesus (pp. 58–59); thinks that it is John speaking in 3:16 (p. 92); holds that the pericope on the woman taken in adultery "is a bit of Synoptic-like material stuck in the middle of John's Gospel" (p. 204); maintains that John 15–17 was likely a later addition (p. 370); holds that there is no certainty on the identity of the "Beloved Disciple" who wrote the Gospel (p. 500).

Other Works on John

Bisagno, John. *The Word Made Flesh.* Waco: Word Books, 1975. 128 pp.

Brief devotional sermons drawn from John 1:1–18. He defends Jesus Christ as the Word, God (p. 12); gives titles for Jesus as the Alphabet of God (p. 18).

Boice, James Montgomery. *Witness and Revelation in the Gospel of John.* Grand Rapids: Zondervan, 1970. 192 pp.

A study of the idea of witness in the Gospel of John.

Burge, Gary M. *Interpreting the Gospel of John.* Grand Rapids: Baker Books, 1992. 185 pp.

Introductory help for the student of John. He defends Johannine authorship (pp. 37ff.), but holds that the text was "edited and reforged by disciples within the Johannine church" (p. 53); calls the fourth Gospel "a fractured text" (p. 74).

Cadman, William H. *The Open Heaven.* Oxford: Blackwell, 1969. 220 pp.

A liberal study of the revelation of God in the Johannine sayings of Jesus. He thinks by His incarnation Jesus became the Son of God (p. 23).

Clark, Gordon H. *The Johannine Logos*. Nutley, NJ: Presbyterian & Reformed, 1972. 90 pp.

A philosophical word study. He defends Johannine authorship (pp. 7ff.); attacks Bultmann's heresy (pp. 36–37).

Ellis, E. Earle. *The World of St. John.* New York: Abingdon, 1965. 96 pp.

A brief study guide. He thinks that John's disciples put the Gospel together in its present form (p. 16); holds that there has been "a considerable interpretive shaping" of Jesus' teaching in the Gospel (p. 29); but he holds that Jesus was both God and man (p. 36).

Gordon, S. D. *Quiet Talks on John's Gospel.* New York: Revell, 1915. 256 pp.

Devotional messages on John's Gospel. "Jesus was God on a wooing errand to the earth" (p. 21); stresses the personal relation to God (p. 57); urges that the way up is the way down (p. 110); discusses five biblical pictures of Jesus (pp. 134f.); stresses "believe-love-obey" (p. 202).

Headlam, Arthur Cayley. *The Fourth Gospel as History*. Oxford: Blackwell, 1948. 106 pp.

He attacks allegorical interpretations and defends actual events recorded in John. He defends Johannine authorship (pp. 32–70); argues that Jesus is Son of God, God incarnate (p. 22).

Johnston, George. *The Spirit-Paraclete in the Gospel of John*. Cambridge: Cambridge University Press, 1970. 192 pp.

A liberal study. He holds to a Second Isaiah (p. 7); thinks that the baptism of Jesus employs mythological language (p. 18); holds that the paraclete was impersonal (p. 81); thinks that John tends to exaggerate (p. 152).

Käsemann, Ernst. *The Testament of Jesus*. Translated by Gerhard Krodel. Philadelphia: Fortress Press, 1968. 99 pp.

He admits he treats a subject he does not understand (p. 1); thinks that John 17 is a literary device of farewell by a dying man (p. 4); holds that John's mythology is an expression of the beginning of dogmatic reflection (p. 23); charges John with "naïve docetism" (p. 26); holds that John "is more fantastic than any other writing of the N.T." (p. 45); Käsemann repudiates the doctrine of the Trinity (p. 48). The fires of hell may change Käsemann's opinions, but not his heart.

Laird, Harold Samuel. *Portraits of Christ in the Gospel of John*. Chicago: Moody, 1936. 126 pp.

Brief devotional meditations on the twenty-one chapters of John. He stresses the eternal deity of Christ (pp. 9f.) and His perfect humanity (pp. 14f.).

MacDuff, J. R. *Noontide at Sychar*. 1877; rpt. Joplin, MO: College Press, 1969. 268 pp.

Warm-hearted exposition of John 4. He provides eloquent descriptions of the countryside as well as of the customs of the Jews and Samaritans.

Morris, Leon. *The Cross in the New Testament*. Grand Rapids: Eerdmans, 1965. "The Cross in the Gospel According to St. John," pp. 144–79.

Morris notes that John never uses the word *faith*, but he uses the verb *to believe* more than 90 times (p. 176).

———. *Jesus Is the Christ*. Grand Rapids: Eerdmans, 1969. 374 pp.

Studies in the theology of John. He discusses the 7 signs and the 7 discourses; Jesus the Son of God (pp. 89ff.); the "I am" sayings (pp. 107ff.).

———. *New Testament Theology*. Grand Rapids: Zondervan, 1986.

"The Gospel of John: the Doctrine of Christ," pp. 225–47.

Moyer, Robert L. *John Three: Sixteen*. Wheaton, IL: Sword of the Lord Publishers, 1938. 127 pp.

Fervent devotional messages on each phrase of the verse. He uses many apt illustrations and quotations; stresses the nature of God and the substitutionary death of Christ.

Murray, Andrew. *Abide in Christ*. New York: Grosset & Dunlap, n.d. 223 pp.

Short devotional meditations drawn from John.

Rainsford, Marcus. *Our Lord Prays for His Own*. Chicago: Moody Press, 1950. 476 pp.

Powerful devotional meditations on the High-Priestly prayer of John 17.

Robertson, Archibald Thomas. *The Divinity of Christ in the Gospel of John*. New York: Revell, 1916. 172 pp.

A devotional defense of the deity of Christ in John. He emphasizes that Christ is "God Only-Begotten" (p. 45); equal with the Father (p. 67) and timeless (p. 83); attacks any theology that is ashamed of the cross (p. 106).

Robinson, William Childs. *Christ—The Bread of Life*. Grand Rapids: Eerdmans, 1950. 190 pp.

Warm-hearted meditations on the Person of Christ: Immanuel, Savior of sinners, Lord of all, God incarnate, the Word, the Shepherd.

Smith, T. C. *Jesus in the Gospel of John*. Nashville: Broadman, 1959. 198 pp.

A study of the Evangelist's purpose. He thinks that the Gospel was written as a defense to the Jews (p. 3); and that an editor has added material (p. 5); refers to "Trito-Isaiah" (p. 41); thinks that the Cana incident had allegorical meaning (p. 107).

Stevens, George B. *The Johannine Theology*. London: Dickinson, 1894. 387 pp.

A liberal study. He notes that John stresses great central truths (p. 2); discusses the idea of God in John (pp. 46ff.), the doctrine of the Logos (pp. 74ff.); the doctrine of sin (pp. 127ff.); the work of salvation (pp. 156ff.).

Swete, Henry Barclay. *The Last Discourse and Prayer of Our Lord.* London: Macmillan, 1913. 187 pp.

Reverent meditations on John 14–17. Although he does not believe in verbal inspiration, he thinks that the words of John 14–17 are as near the actual words of the Lord as memory makes possible (p. x); stresses the imminent return of Christ (pp. 8–9); and the fact that He is the incarnate Way to God (p. 14); stresses that no spiritual fruit can be produced apart from the Incarnate Word (p. 77); holds that the knowledge of God which is life "is more than the intellectual acceptance of a true faith" (p. 163).

Van Ryn, August. *Meditations in John.* Chicago: Moody, 1949. 205 pp.

Brief devotional studies from John. He stresses that the theme of John is belief in Christ as the Son of God (pp. 11ff.); lists a number of "sevens" in John (pp. 16f.); discusses three doors (pp. 31ff.); three days (pp. 41ff.); "I am—seven great claims" (pp. 43ff.).

Zeller, George W., and Renald E. Showers. *The Eternal Sonship of Christ.* Neptune, NJ: Loizeaux, 1993. 126 pp.

A formal defense of the doctrine. They defend the deity and pre-existence of the Son (pp. 17–22); list numerous Scriptures that teach the eternal sonship (pp. 26ff., 36ff.) They cite defenders of the doctrine such as Spurgeon, Charles Hodge, Warfield, Walvoord, and others (pp. 110ff.).

Zodhiates, Spiros. *Was Christ God?* Grand Rapids: Eerdmans, 1966. 350 pp.

A formal exegesis of the Greek text of John 1:1–18. He argues for the reading "only begotten God" in John 1:18. He stresses the fact that Jesus Christ was not merely "divine" but was God Himself (pp. 107ff.).

Works on Jesus Christ

Erickson, Millard. *The Word Became Flesh.* Grand Rapids: Baker, 1991. 663 pp.

A formal defense of the incarnate nature of Christ.

Geldenhuys, J. Norval. *Supreme Authority.* Grand Rapids: Eerdmans, 1953. 128 pp.

He holds that the Lord Jesus Christ is that supreme authority for all believers.

Guthrie, Donald. *New Testament Theology*. Downers Grove, IL: Inter-Varsity Press, 1981. 1064 pp.

Christology (pp. 219–509).

Hunt, T. W. *The Mind of Christ*. Nashville: Broadman & Holman, 1995. 183 pp.

See especially "The Lifestyle of Christ" and following. (pp. 39ff.).

Large, James. *Two Hundred and Eighty Titles and Symbols of Christ*. 1888; rpt. Grand Rapids: Baker Book House, 1959. 486 pp.

Liddon, Henry P. *The Divinity of Our Lord*. London: Longmans, Green, and Co., 1892. 585 pp.

A fervent scholarly defense of the deity of the Lord Jesus.

Marshall, I. Howard. *The Origins of New Testament Christology*. Downers Grove, IL: Inter-Varsity, 1976. 132 pp.

A conservative investigation.

Morgan, G. Campbell. *The Crises of the Christ*. New York: Revell, 1903, 1936. 477 pp.

The high points of the life of Christ: His birth, baptism, temptation, transfiguration, Crucifixion, Resurrection, and Ascension.

Morris, Leon. *The Lord From Heaven*. Grand Rapids: Eerdmans, 1958. 112 pp.

New Testament teaching on the deity and humanity of Christ.

Owen, John. *The Glory of Christ*. Chicago: Moody Press, 1949, rpt. 285 pp.

Devotional meditations.

Patterson, Alexander. *The Greater Life and Work of Christ*. Chicago: Moody Press, n.d. 408 pp.

From eternity past to eternity future.

Smith, Wilbur M. *The Supernaturalness of Christ*. Boston: W. A. Wilde Company, 1944. 235 pp.

A defense of the divine nature of Christ.

Stalker, James. *Imago Christi: The Example of Jesus Christ*. 1889; rpt. Greenville, SC: BJU Press, 2002. 230 pp.

Fervent meditations.

Van Bruggen, Jakob. *Jesus the Son of God*. Grand Rapids: Baker Books, 1996. 307 pp.

A formal defense of the doctrine.

Vos, Geerhardus. *The Self-Disclosure of Jesus*. Grand Rapids: Eerdmans, 1926, 1953. 311 pp.

Walvoord, John. *Jesus Christ Our Lord.* Chicago; Moody Press, 1969. 318 pp.

A conservative Christology organized on major topics, such as His incarnation, person, life, suffering, death, Resurrection, and others.

Warfield, Benjamin B. *The Lord of Glory*. Grand Rapids: Zondervan, 1907. 332 pp.

A study of the names and titles of Christ.

———. *The Person and Work of Christ*. Philadelphia: Presbyterian & Reformed, 1970, rpt. 575 pp.

A conservative study of Christology.

Whyte, Alexander. *The Walk, Conversation, and Character of Jesus Christ Our Lord*. New York: Fleming H. Revell Company, 1905. 340 pp.

A warm-hearted portrait of the beautiful character of the Lord Jesus.

Encyclopedia Articles and Dictionaries

Barabas, Steven. "John, Gospel of." *The New International Dictionary of the Bible*. J. D. Douglas and Merrill Tenney, eds. Grand Rapids: Zondervan, 1987. pp. 533–36.

Biedermann, Hans. "Cross." *Dictionary of Symbolism*. New York: Facts on File, 1989, 1992. 465 pp. pp. 81–84.

Burge, Gary M. "John, Theology of." *Evangelical Dictionary of Biblical Theology*. Walter A. Elwell, ed. pp. 423–27.

Baker's Dictionary of Theology. Everett F. Harrison, ed. "Cross," p. 152; "Jesus," pp. 297f. Grand Rapids: Baker Book House, 1978. 566 pp.

The New Unger's Bible Dictionary. R. K. Harrison, ed. "John, The Gospel of," pp. 700–02.

Holman Bible Dictionary, Trent C. Butler, ed. "Ethics," pp. 441–44.

Marshall, I. Howard. "Johannine Theology," *International Standard Bible Encyclopedia*, II, pp. 1081–91.

Metzger, Bruce M., and Michael Coogan. *The Oxford Companion to the Bible*. New York: Oxford University Press, 1993. "John, The Gospel According to," pp. 373–77.

Morris, Leon. "John, Gospel According to," *International Standard Bible Encyclopedia*, II, pp. 1098–1107.

New Dictionary of Biblical Theology. Alexander et al., eds. "The Johannine Writings," pp. 132–36; A. J. Köstenberger, "John," pp. 280–85.

Turner, G. A. "John, Gospel of." *Zondervan Pictorial Encyclopedia of the Bible*, III, pp. 657–74.

Bibles and Testaments

Aland, Barbara, et al. *The Greek New Testament*. 4th rev. ed. Stuttgart: Deutsche Bibelgesellschaft, 1966, 1993. 918 pp.

The Apologetics Study Bible. Ted Cabal, ed. Nashville: Holman Bible Publishers, 2007. 2008 pp. plus maps.

The Holy Bible: English Standard Version. Wheaton, IL: Crossway Bibles, 2002. 1328 pp.

The International Inductive Study Bible. NASB. Eugene, OR: Harvest House Publishers, 1977. 2206 pp.

Kittel, Rudolf. *Biblia Hebraica*. Stuttgart: Württembergische Bibelanstalt, 1937, 1954. 1434 pp.

Metzger, Bruce M. *A Textual Commentary on the Greek New Testament*. United Bible Societies, 1971. 775 pp.

Moulton, W. F., and A. S. Geden. *A Concordance to the Greek Testament*. Edinburgh: T. & T. Clark, 1897, 1953. 1033 pp.

Nestle, Eberhard, and Kurt Aland. *Novum Testamentum Graece*. 26th ed. Stuttgart: Deutsche Bibelstiftung, 1898, 1979. 779, 78 (intro.) pp.

Rahlfs, Alfred. *Septuaginta*. Stuttgart: Württembergische Bibelanstalt, 1935. 2 vols.; 1184, 941 pp.

Ryrie, Charles Caldwell. *The Ryrie Study Bible*. Chicago: Moody Press, 1976. 2006 pp.

Scofield, C. I. *The Scofield Study Bible*. New York: Oxford University Press, 1909, 1945. 1362 pp.

Westcott, B. F., and F. J. A. Hort. *The Greek New Testament*. Peabody, MA: Hendrickson Publishers, 2007, rpt. 893 pp.

Other Works Cited

Alon, Azaria. *The Natural History of the Land of the Bible*. New York: Paul Hamlyn, 1969. 276 pp.

Berkhof, L. *Systematic Theology*. Grand Rapids: Eerdmans, 1941. 784 pp.

Biblical Viewpoint. "Focus on John." Vol. XXXIV, No. 1, April, 2000.

Bright, John. *The Kingdom of God*. New York: Abingdon-Cokesbury Press, 1953. 288 pp.

A liberal discussion.

Currie, Robin, and Stephen Hyslop, *The Letter and the Scroll*. Washington, D.C.: National Geographic, 2009. 336 pp.

Custer, Stewart. *A Treasury of New Testament Synonyms*. Greenville, SC: Bob Jones University Press, 1975. 143 pp.

———. *Stones of Witness: Images of the Holy Land*. Greenville, SC: BJU Press, 2002. 236 pp.

Edersheim, Alfred. *Sketches of Jewish Social Life*. Grand Rapids: Eerdmans, 1950. 342 pp.

Gafni, Shlomo S. *The Glory of Jerusalem*. Jerusalem: The Jerusalem Publishing House, 1978. 128 pp.

Color photographs.

Guthrie, Donald. *New Testament Theology*. Downers Grove, IL: Inter-Varsity Press, 1981. 1064 pp.

Each section deals with the teaching of the Johannine literature, pp. 130ff.; 158ff.; 193ff.; 222ff.; 230ff., etc.

Kaiser, Walter C., P. H. Davids, F. F. Bruce, and M. T. Brauch. *Hard Sayings of the Bible*. Downers Grove, IL: InterVarsity, 1996. pp. 490–510.

They discuss the Word and the Trinity (pp. 490ff.); being born of water and the Spirit (pp. 495f.).

Kempis, Thomas A. *The Imitation of Christ*. New York; Grosset & Dunlap, rpt. 352 pp.

Mazar, Benjamin. *The Mountain of the Lord*. New York: Doubleday, 1975. 304 pp.

Archaeological descriptions and photographs of Jerusalem.

McRay, John. *Archaeology and the New Testament*. Grand Rapids: Baker Book House, 1991. 432 pp.

Lavishly illustrated.

Morgan, G. Campbell. *Living Messages of the Books of the Bible*. Vol. II, New Testament. "The Message of John," pp. 56–73.

A loving analysis.

Murray, Andrew. *Abide in Christ*. New York: Grosset & Dunlap, n.d. 223 pp.

Devotional meditations for a month drawn from John 15:4 and other related passages.

———. *Like Christ*. Philadelphia: Henry Altimus Company, n.d. 282 pp.
Devotional meditations for a month drawn from John, I John, and related Scripture passages.

———. *With Christ in the School of Prayer*. New York: Fleming H. Revell, n.d. 274 pp.

Owen, G. Frederick. *The Shepherd Psalm of Palestine*. Grand Rapids: Eerdmans, 1958. 84 pp.
Gravure photographs.

Pache, René. *The Person and Work of the Holy Spirit*. Chicago: Moody Press, 1954. 223 pp.

Swete, Henry Barclay. *The Holy Spirit in the New Testament*. Grand Rapids: Baker Book House, 1964. 417 pp.

Tasker, R. V. G., *The Biblical Doctrine of the Wrath of God*. London: Tyndale Press, 1951. 48 pp.

Thomas, W. H. Griffith. *The Holy Spirit of God*. Grand Rapids: Eerdmans, 1913, 1964. "The Holy Spirit in the Fourth Gospel," pp. 59–67.

Thubron, Colin. *Jerusalem*. Amsterdam: Time-Life International, 1976. 200 pp.

Torrey, R. A. *What the Bible Teaches*. New York: Revell, 1933. 539 pp.

Walvoord, John F. *The Holy Spirit*. Wheaton, IL: Van Kampen Press, 1954. 275 pp.

Warfield, Benjamin B. *The Inspiration and Authority of the Bible*. Philadelphia: Presbyterian & Reformed Publishing Company, 1948. 442 pp.